Summer on the Hill

Paintings by Philip Zuchman

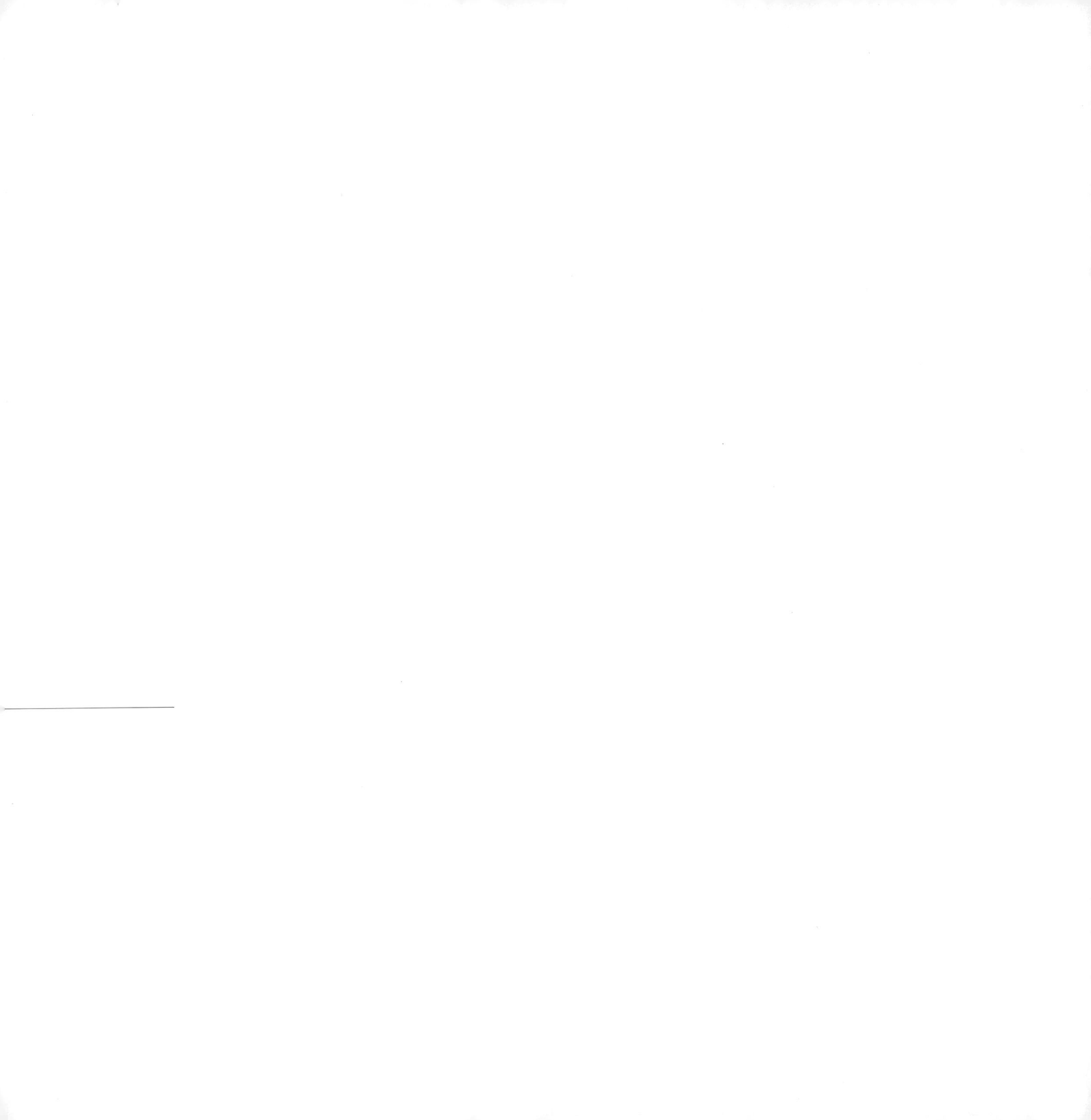

Summer on the Hill

Paintings by Philip Zuchman

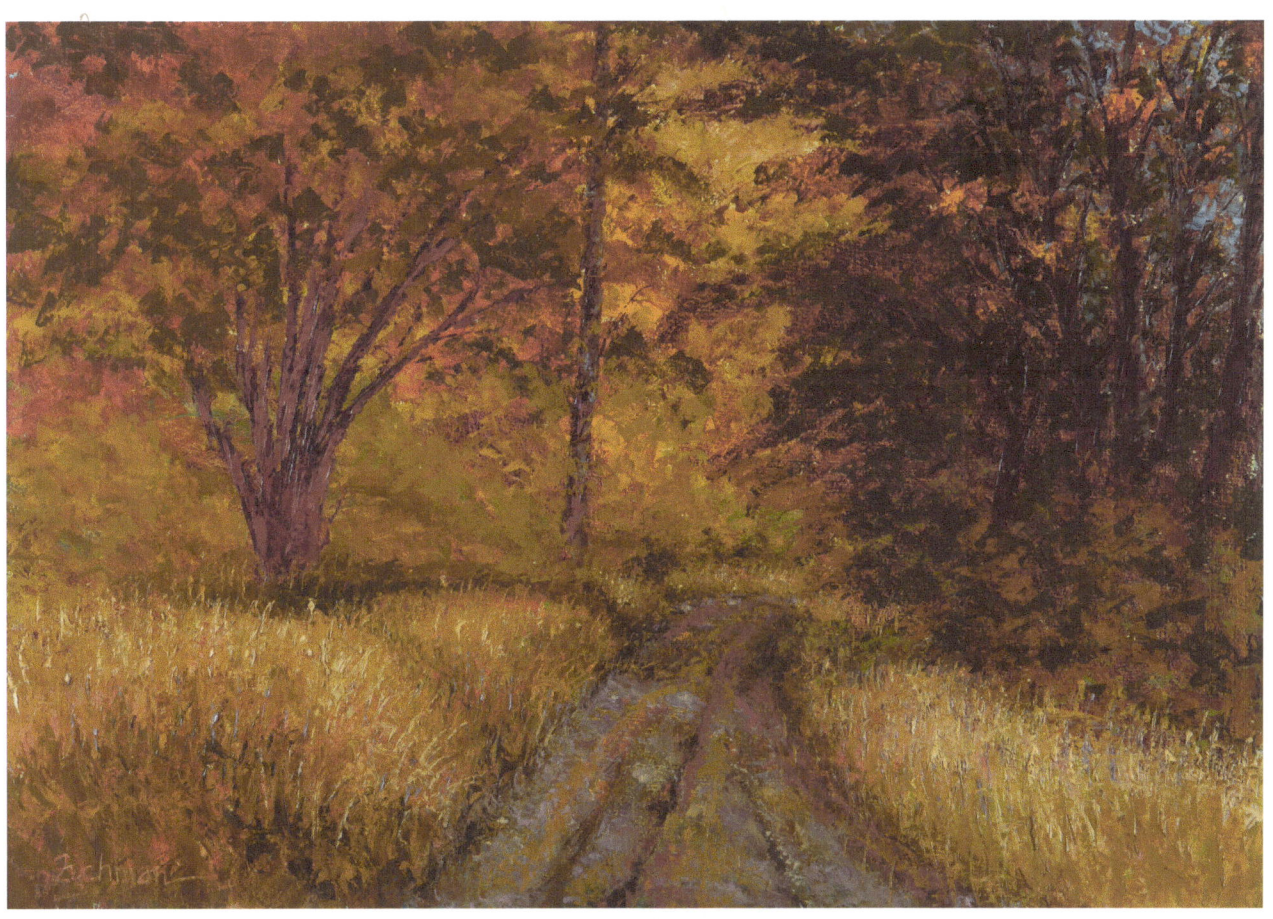

ABINGDON SQUARE PUBLISHING

New York

Summer on the Hill
is published by
Abingdon Square Publishing Ltd.
463 West Street, Suite G122
New York, NY 10014 USA
www.abingdonsquarepublishing.com

Book Design: Abingdon Square Publishing
Cover Art: *High Ledges Wildlife Sanctuary* © Philp Zuchman, 2011

ISBN 978-0-9830762-3-0
Library of Congress Control Number: 2012934190

First Printing: March 2012
Printed in the United States of America

Summer on the Hill:
the paintings of Philip Zuchman

Why, you might ask, would an accomplished artist who has traveled the world, designed, built and paddled a 14 foot kayak 2,000 miles to the Carolina Sea Islands, lived in, painted and exhibited his work in many glorious places on several continents, why would such an artist return year after year for more than a quarter of a century, set up his easel every morning, walk from where he resides and set about capturing something that he, and everyone else who passes by the same place a thousand times in the course of a year, also sees? I have often seen Philip as I pass the same way as he and often wondered why he has stopped here. Nice enough trees, hills, meadows, bends in the road, clouds and such, but really, the countryside abounds in such stuff, why this stuff? Why does this man seem so modest in his choices? Why isn't he more, well, artistic?

From one year to the next Philip employs the same art materials and tools (painting knives), the same size and format to work on. What's going on? Surely he knows the world of art in these same fifty years that he has been a practicing artist, has experimented with every material, at every scale and served every purpose and transgressed every boundary, alarming and bedazzling collectors, offended ordinary citizens, perplexed even more; why has this man not been swayed by this fantastic cavalcade of exhibitionists? Why does this man continue to take his easel out each morning, find a rather pleasant but unexceptional line of sight, and then, work away for several hours painting a "picture?" A picture! Even this apogee art form in Western culture, a picture, seems to have been eclipsed by people stuffing animals, shooting themselves and others, setting things on fire, digging pits, smearing themselves with this and that. Yet, Philip seems quite content, even excited about painting a picture.

Lots of people can be seen with their paper and paints creating charming pictures of lovely sights. But, Philip's work is not charming. If what he sees is not conventionally artistic, and what he chooses to include in his painting is not particularly charming, and the degree of transformation that he allows himself is modest, just what is this man about? What is he seeing that brings him back to look and look again, year after year, in the same fields, among the same roads, every day, in all kinds of weather – religiously bent over his work?

Religiously, Philip attends to his work and to the earth – religiously. Don't for a moment mistake Philip's religious intensity for religion's religiosity. Philip is an artist and by that I mean a person who chooses to love what he happens to be devoted to. An artist as in a person who creates the world he desires to live within rather than endures living in a world that is handed down to him and required to love.

Philip is an artist who throughout his life has taken pains to carve out an informed, thoughtful, reflective and hard won life. Not out of whole prepared cloth, but bit by bit he has handcrafted each one of the elements of his life. Everything that he invites to remain in his scheme of values, everything that becomes a component of his home, his teaching, every artifact he creates; from walking sticks to hand crafted wines, to his paintings, all matter. Really matter. For when each thing is treated as if it truly matters, each thing truly comes to matter. This is the woven fabric of an artist's life; whatever the material; for an artist, everything matters and every stroke that goes into its fabrication matters. This is both the material and the method of art: wherein every thing and every gesture matters. As best as he is able, and at substantial cost over the years, that is a fair description of Phil's life.

The appreciation of Philip's stance in life will lead to an appreciation of Philip's art and the answer to our original question, why does Philip paint the way he does?

What do we see when we actually look at Philip's work? Unsurprisingly, we see landscapes. More or less than what he has been looking at all the while. And this is exactly his art; the more and the less than what he sees. We'll examine the "more" portion first, then the "less."

The color shift in his palette is the first quality that strikes one. And it is here in his choice of color schemes that Philip is most inventive. The closely matched greens of mid summer are now replaced with a wider range of tones and tints. And these in turn are now given to us in layers of contrasting hues and saturations. The effect of this broadening and layering is to animate the flat surface of the painting to equal the vibrancy of the constantly changing light, the twirling shift of surfaces of the millions of leaves, grasses and clouds, all within yawning depths of space of nature just as it is. The scarlet and rose and mauve and sepia and chartreuse and cerulean of Philip's palette replace nature's own infinite variations on green. And how nature forms its own endless variety of twigs, pebbles, leaves and grasses is now replaced by Philip's wide range of textured application of paint. Smears, glazes, washes, impastos, scumbles, blotches and the like build an uneven surface of the painting making the whole pulsate, again, like the shimmering of the light on any portion of nature's beauty.

Looking a bit closer, we might observe that the heavily applied textures create definite patterns and rhythms that join the various areas of the painting into melodic lines. In fact, if one subtracted all the color from the painting and had it only in one hue, the ripples and eddies across the surface would still provide us with poetry enough.

So now we can begin to see in comparing Philip's landscape painting with what he must see of nature. We can now begin to assemble a conception of what Philip's "more" is. He has substituted the biologic and optical fantasia of nature for the rhyming, musical, poetic underpinnings that all creation coheres around. The manifest world is the here and now concretization of universal patterning, and it is the observing of the patterning tendencies of all creation; leaves and clouds and grasses that Philip's seeing reveals. And it is of course just this similarity of cohering musicality that we share with the rest of creation that allows us to be moved when we encounter the rising sun, the rising of the moon, and the setting of each in their necessary turn.

We now come to the paintings' composition – where the things the artist has chosen to include and where he places them for the effect desired. And so we come to the "less" of his work.

Much like poetry, that is often observed to be the most compressed of language forms, Philip's paintings are heroic in what they exclude from nature's endless cornucopia.

And much like Odysseus, who had himself tied to the mast of his ship so he would not be seduced by the Siren's enchanting songs, as he passed by their menacing waters, the hardest task of an artist is not so much as to invent alternative worlds to the world given, but not to be so overwhelmed by the matchless beauties of this world, and so be mesmerized, paralyzed, and become sated just by looking and listening and looking. Here Philip is severe. Rather than the seductions of dramatic foreshortenings, steep angles, stunning close ups, shocking twists of limbs and pathways, opulent meadows bursting with this color and that, Philip quiets the tumultuous mess down by giving us nature head on, intense but calm.

In Philip's world the closely matched rhythms and quiet melodies keep coming forth, remarkably taking up hardly any space at all. We seem to have room for more and more of seeing his work without ever becoming sated by overly rich fare. Viewing a series of his paintings is something like dining on an array of gorgeously made finger food at a tapas or sushi bar.

Like many artists who are disinterested in creating a single work that is intended to wow and exhaust your appetite for anything more, Philip's work is best seen in large numbers. Because any one painting offers the viewer modest innovation from given nature, when seen as a swarm of paintings we can better appreciate the many subtleties of his highly sensitive seeing and actually quite inventive variations. And it is the high number and the refined subtlety of his variations that together define his contribution to what nature offers him to build upon. Beholding an entire exhibition of his work, we now notice the entire shifting consciousness or lens with which Philip views this evanescent world. Within this broader scope we now see the world quietly humming, the humming of course now transposed to chords of color and rhythms of textures, modulations in volume now become variations in saturation in hue. A season's work now seen side by side, provides the viewer with another layer of meaning and reward; for now we experience the evolving personalities of nature, each different quality of light evincing yet another facet of personality embedded within nature's infinite complexity.

So, to the question posed at the outset of this essay: why does Philip return year after year to the same subject matter? We can now answer; have you not seen the hundreds of takes Monet invested in his water lily pond? Or the hours on end that Cezanne gave over to his apples and pears, or Rembrandt spent over the course of his lifetime staring at his own face? An artist is the type of person who never exhausts his fascination with the endless permutations not only of nature, but the themes and variations that come to mind – an open and available mind, upon witnessing this glorious world.

Peter London
Davis, California, 2011

Peter London, MFA, Ed.D., is Chancellor Professor Emeritus, at the University of Massachusetts Dartmouth. He is a Distinguished Fellow of the National Art Education Association, Honorary Doctorate, Maryland Institute College of Art, and is an exhibiting artist whose work is in national and international private and public collections. Retired from the university, Peter continues to teach and lecture internationally. He is the author of a number of books on art and art education, including, "No More Secondhand Art", and "Drawing Closer to Nature." www peterlondon.us

Summer on the Hill

Paintings by Philip Zuchman

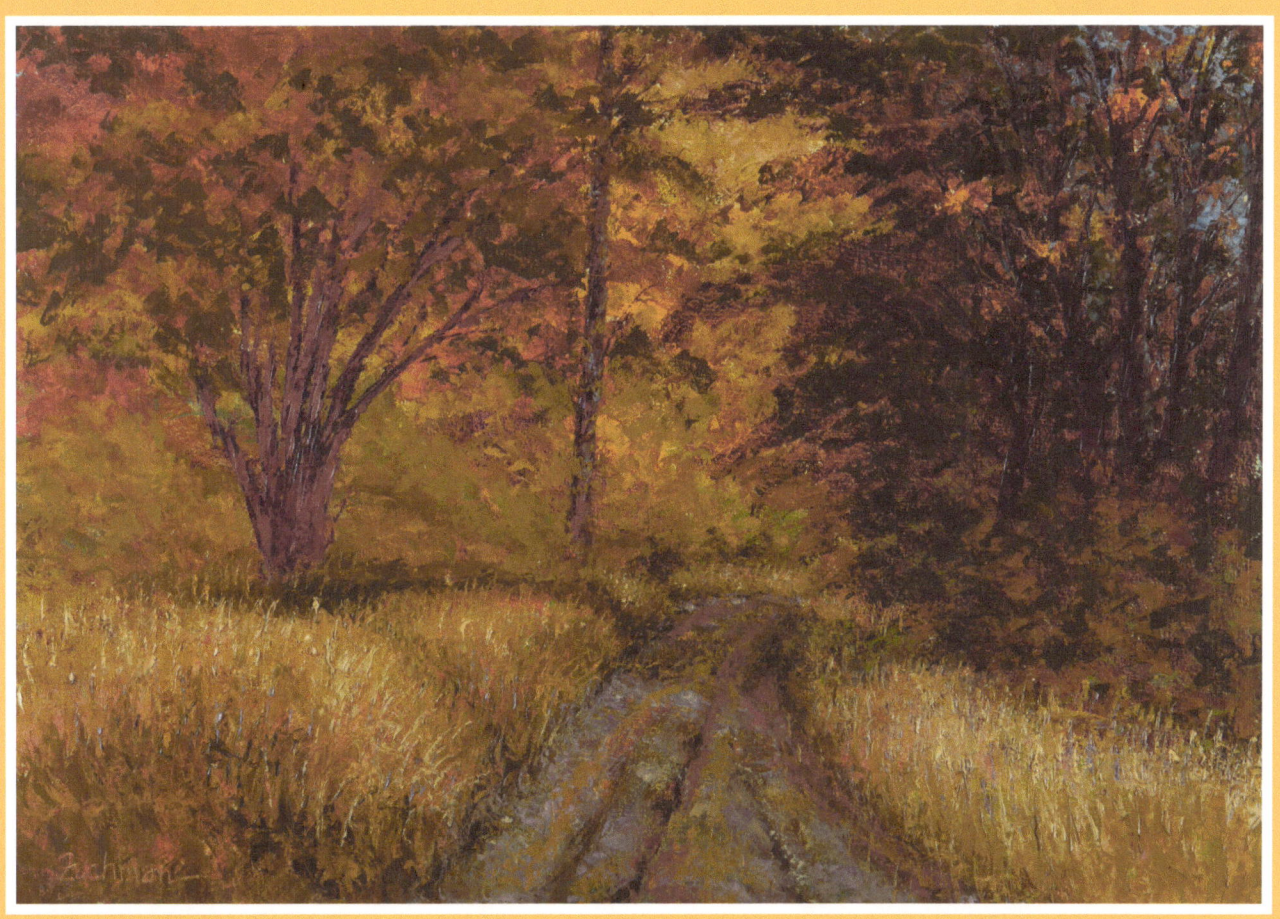

High Ledges Wildlife Sanctuary

Mount Snow From Patten Hill

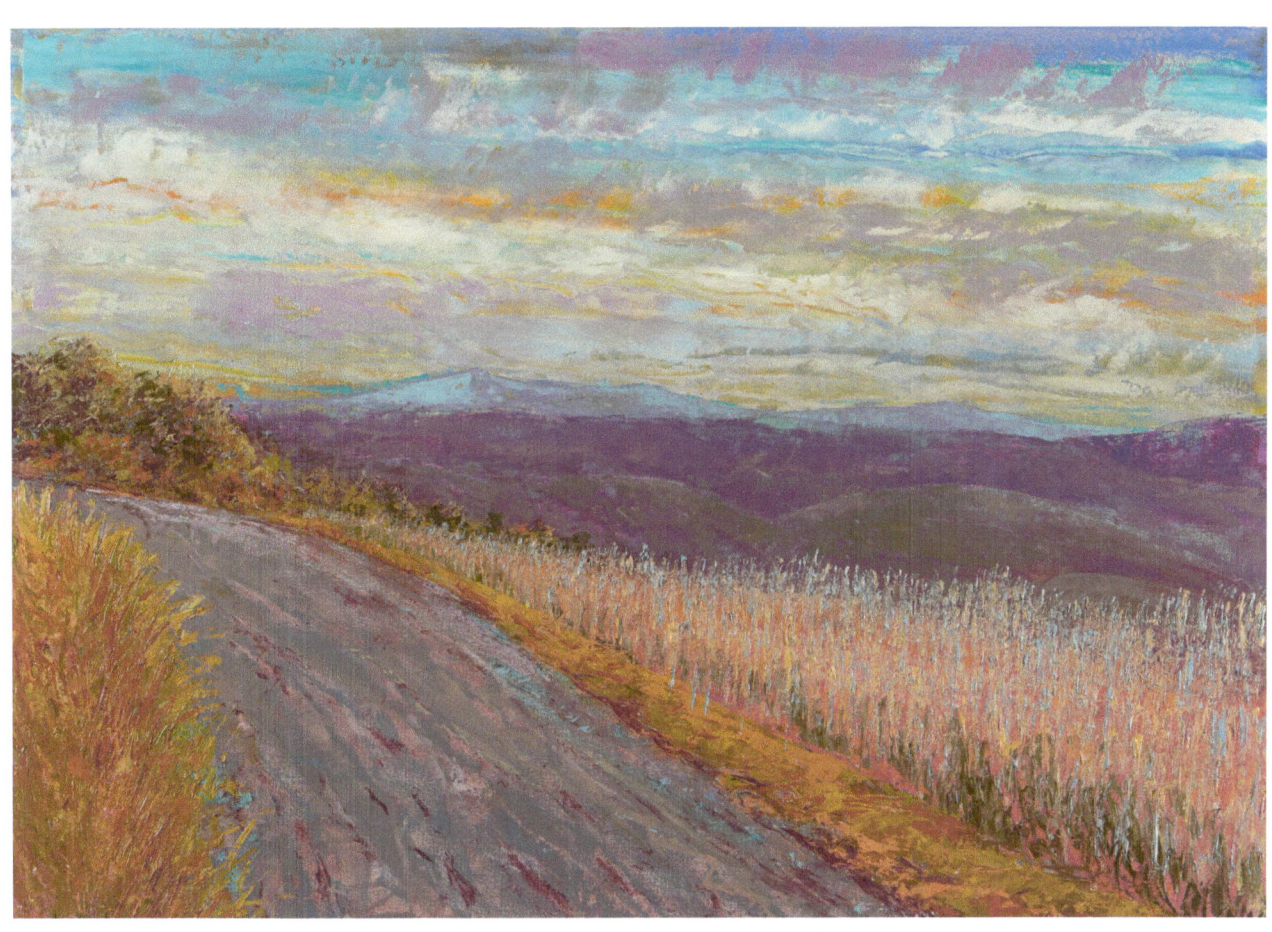

What art means is not more important
than what art is.

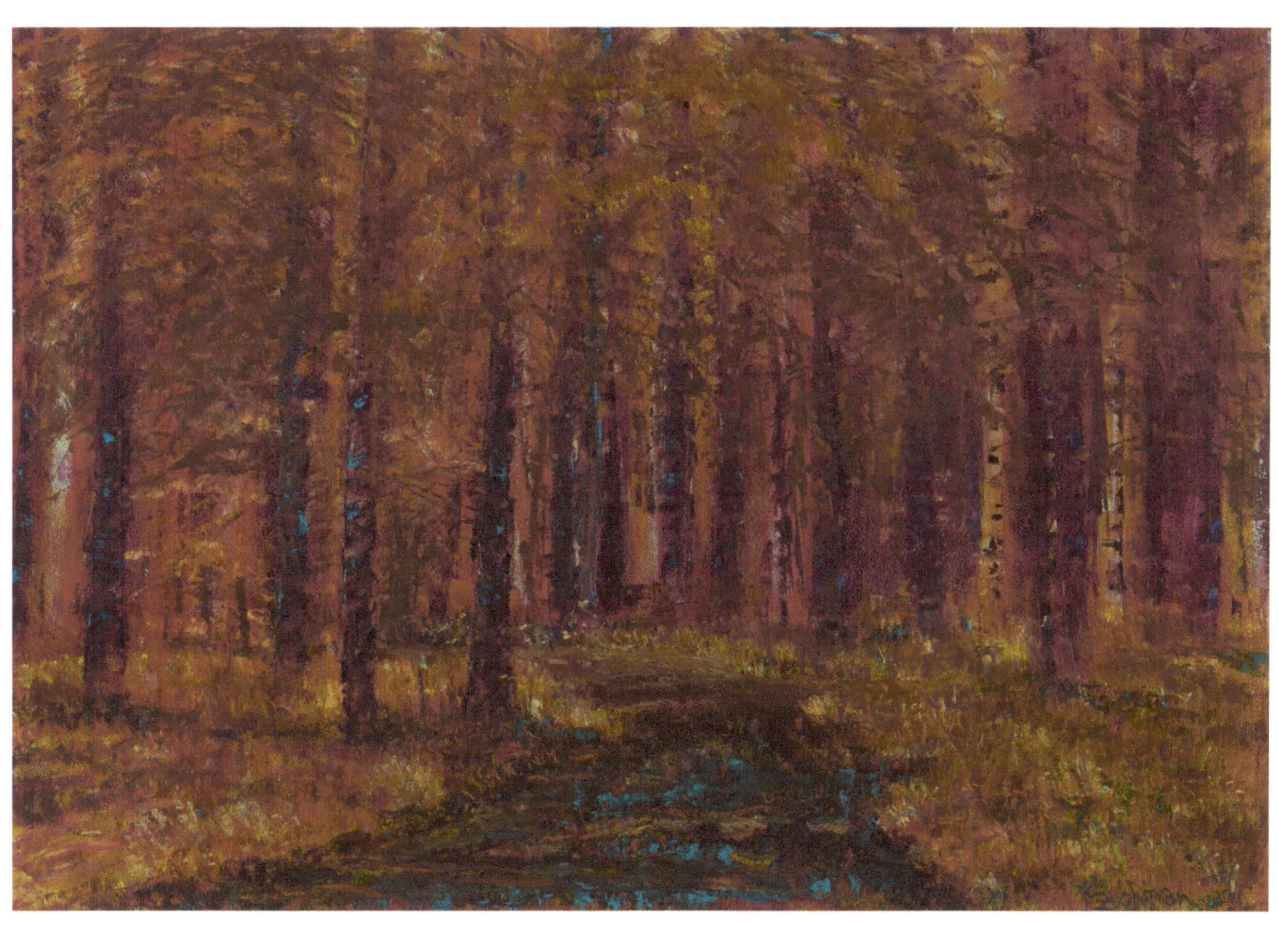

Apple Orchard at Truesdell's #1

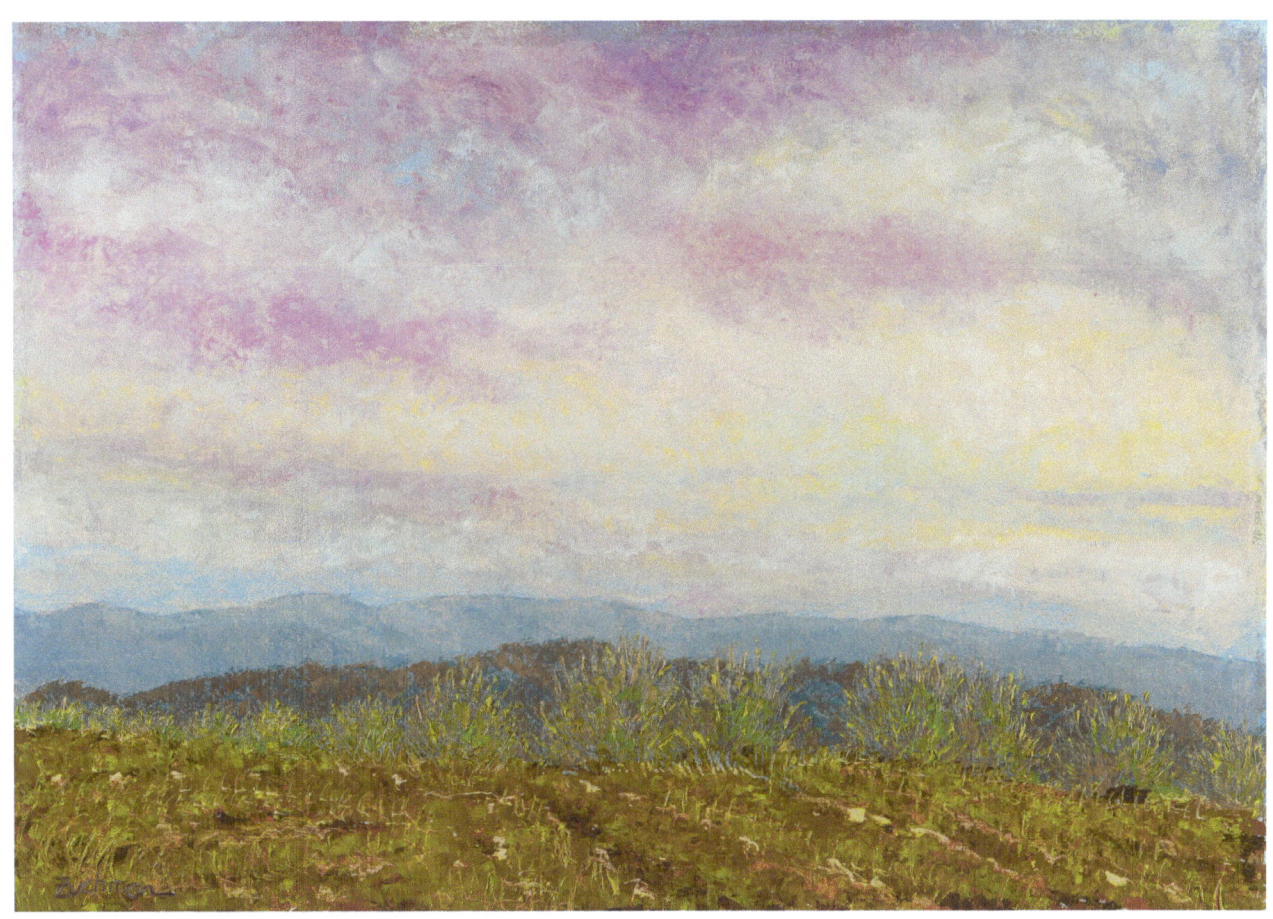

I paint from chaos to order.

Northeast Vista

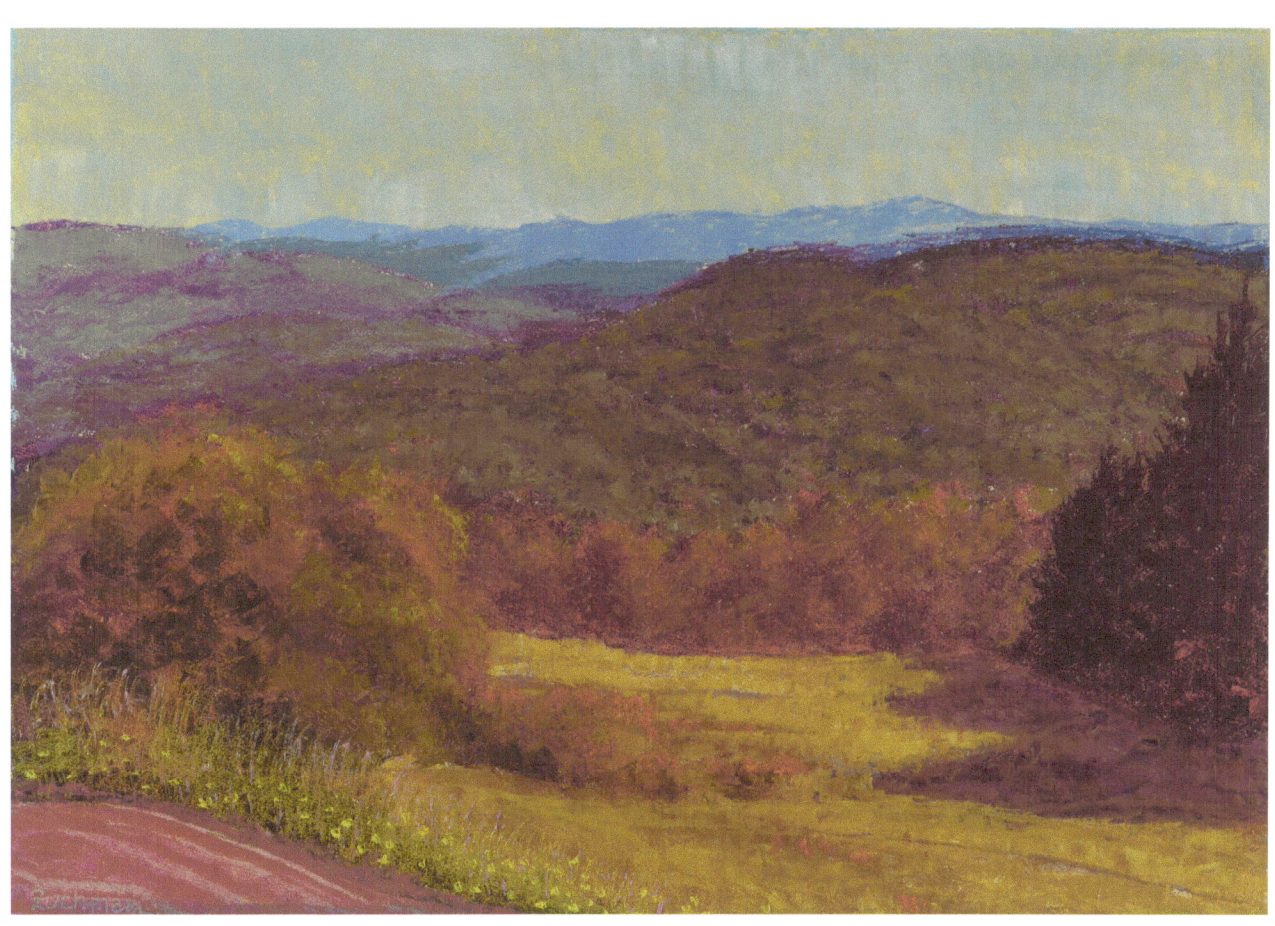

Tractor Trail

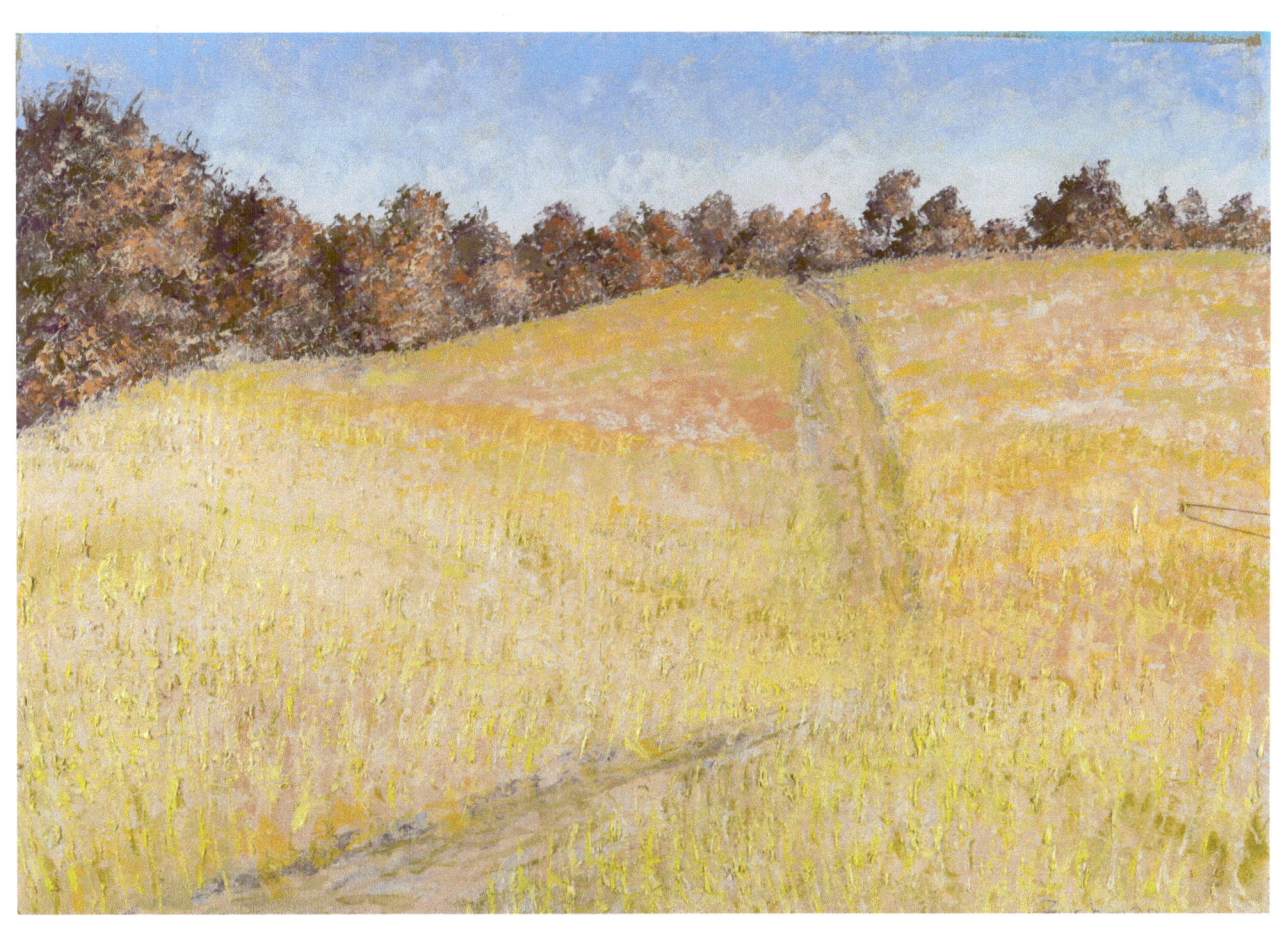

*The paintings I recognize as my own
are the ones I haven't painted yet.*

Above the Watershed

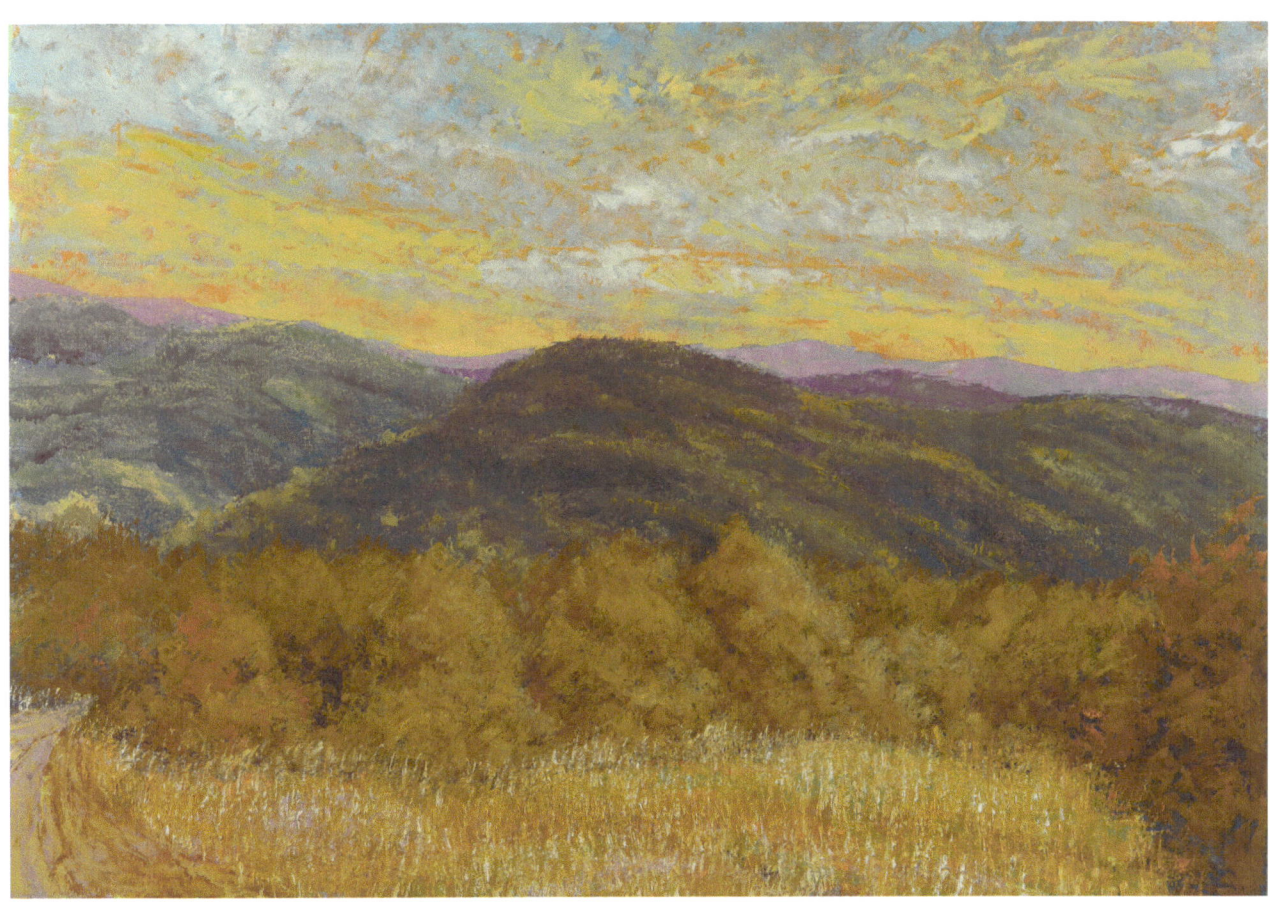

Swamp At Goldswaithe's #1

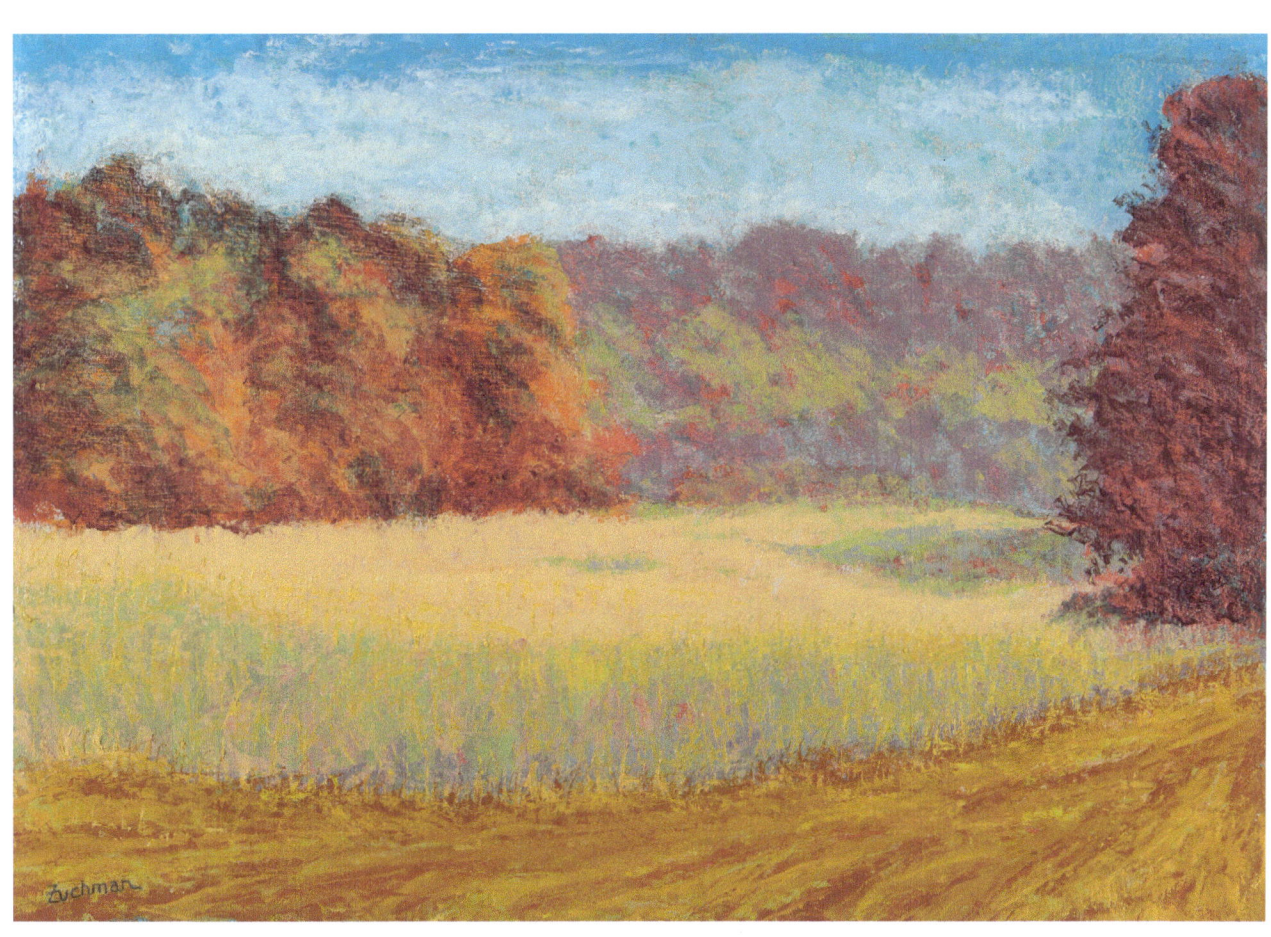

In every work of art I make is truth,
ambiguity and falsehood.

Sanctuary Meadow #2

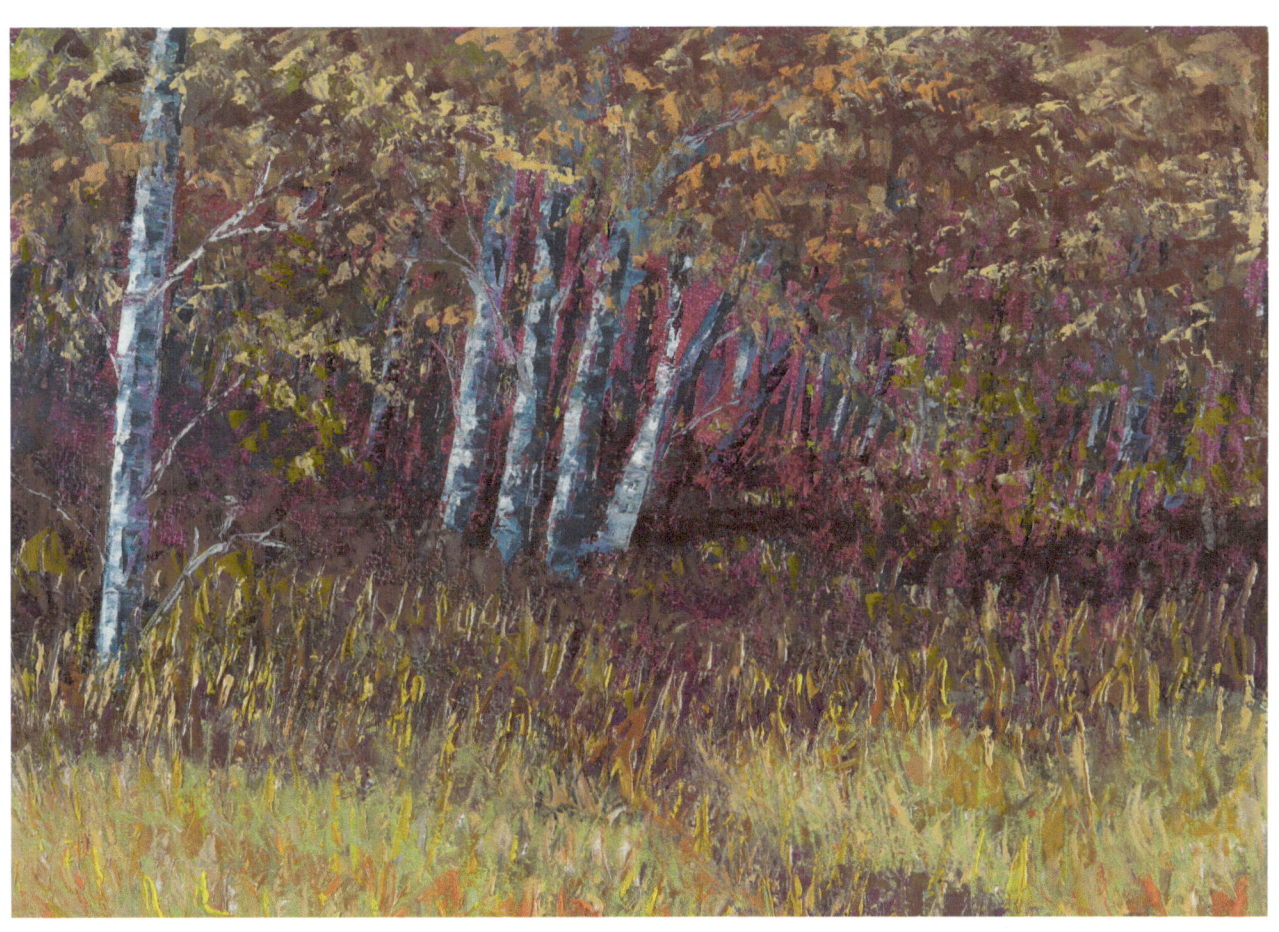

Patten Road

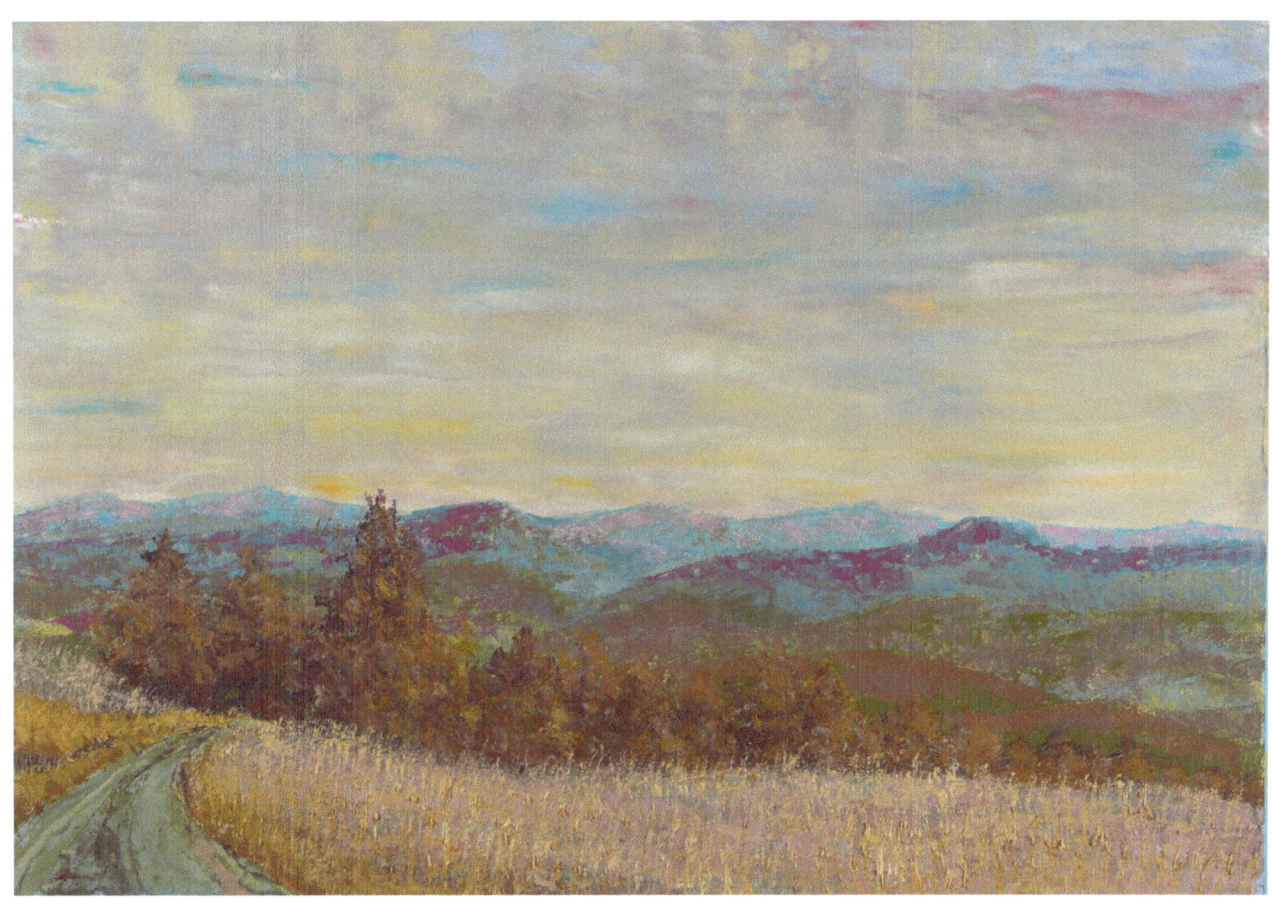

The salsa needs spice, the eggs need beating.
This is my aesthetic.

Swamp at Goldswaithe's #2

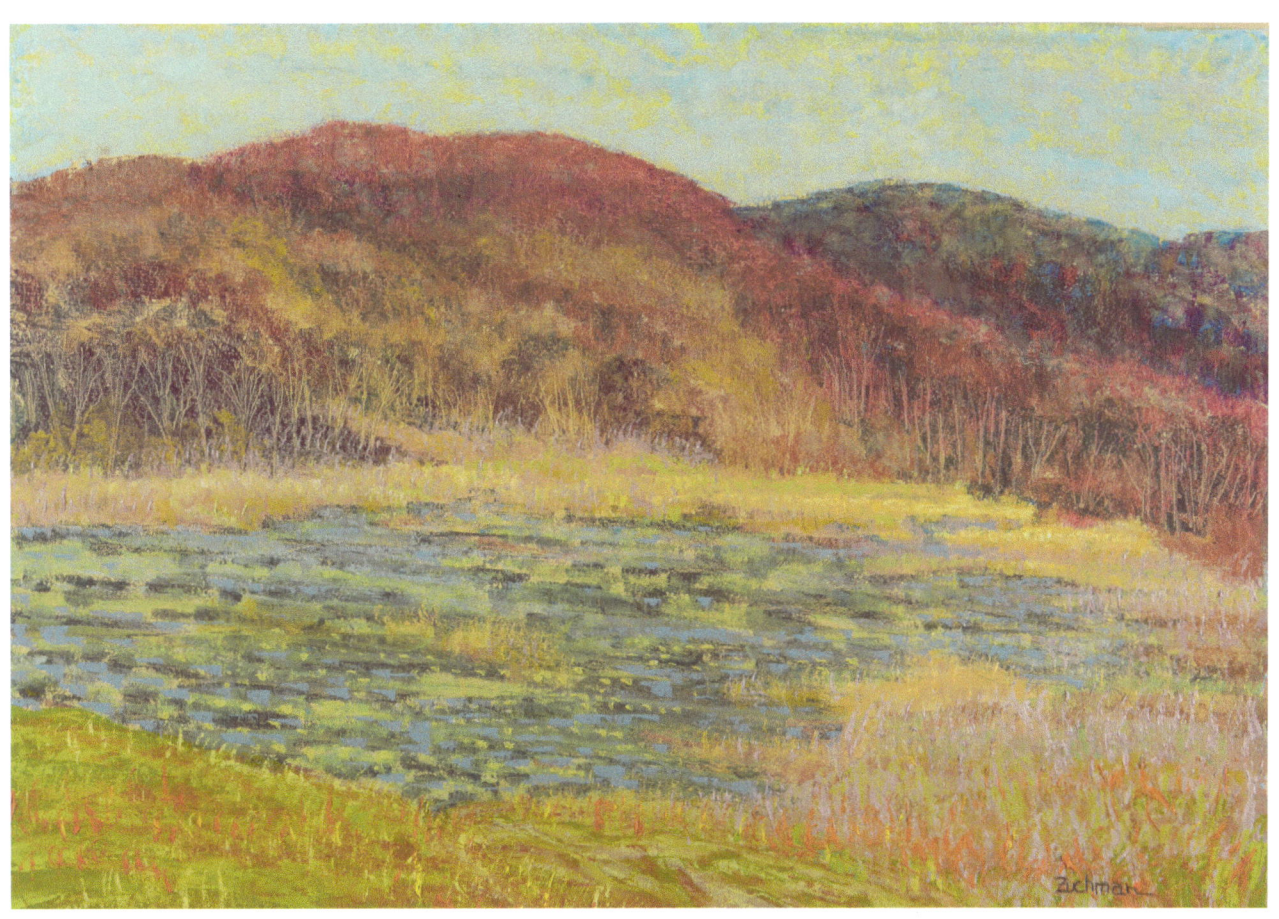

Pioneer Valley from Florida

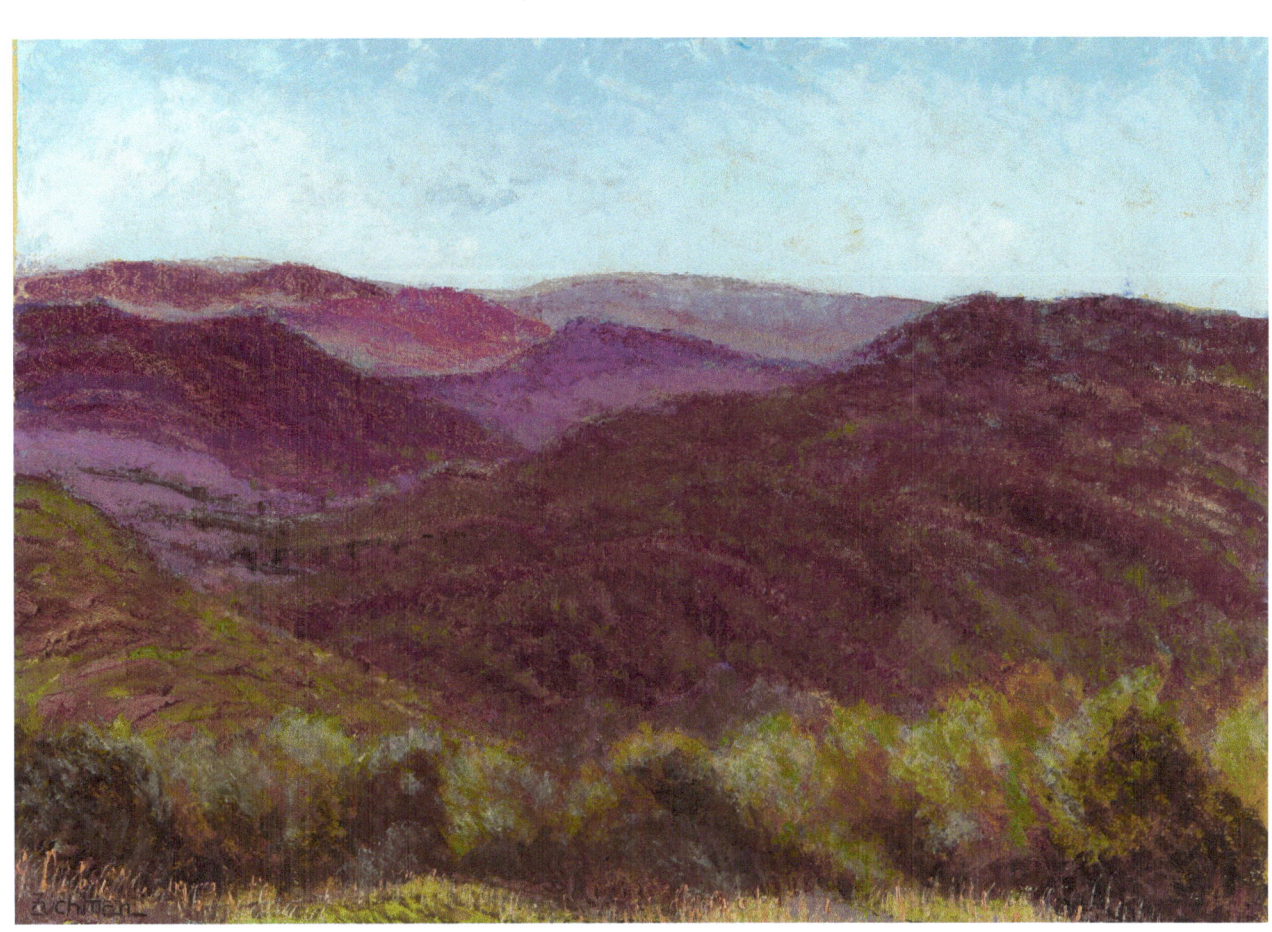

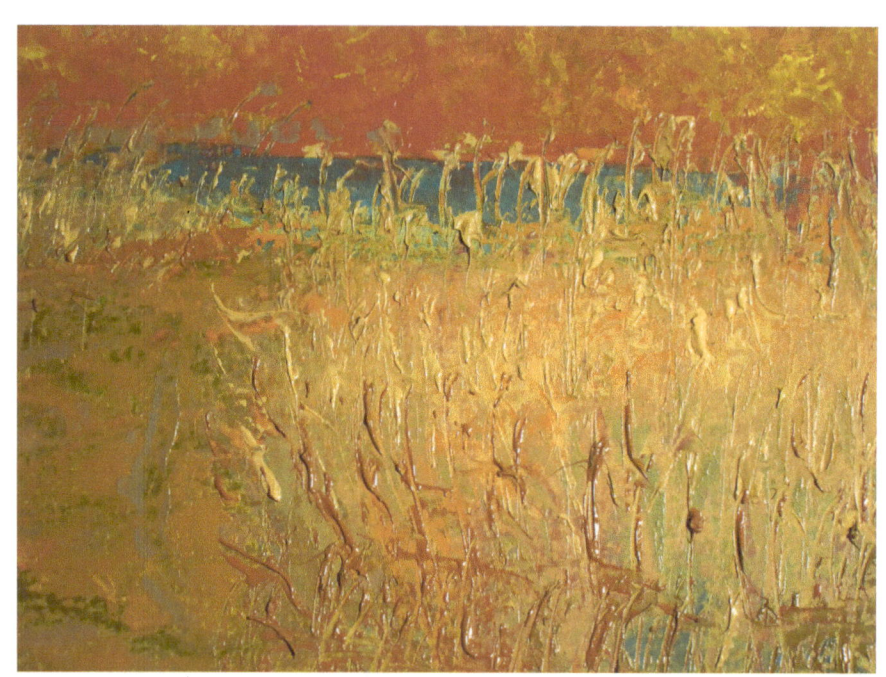

In the Mow

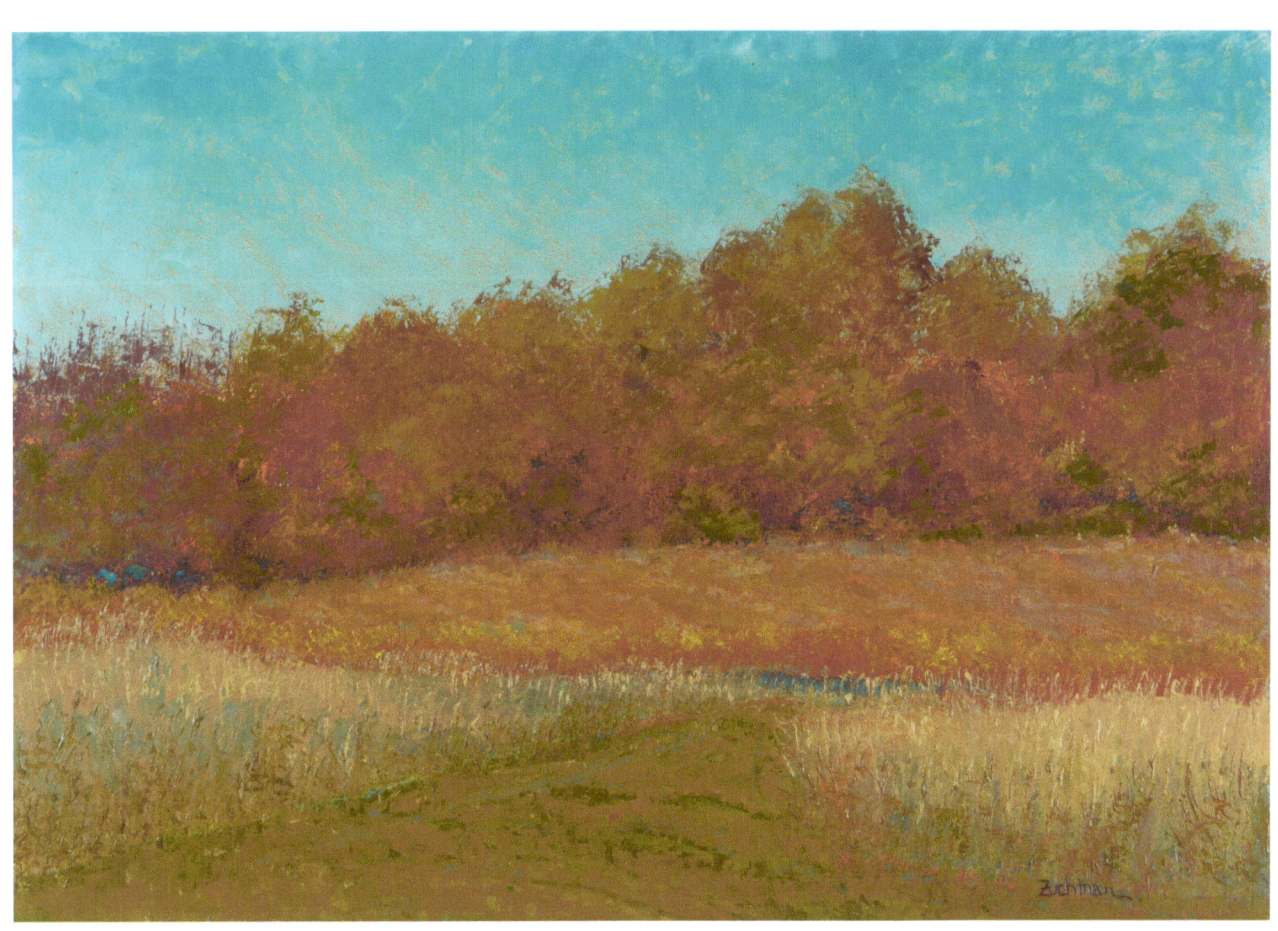

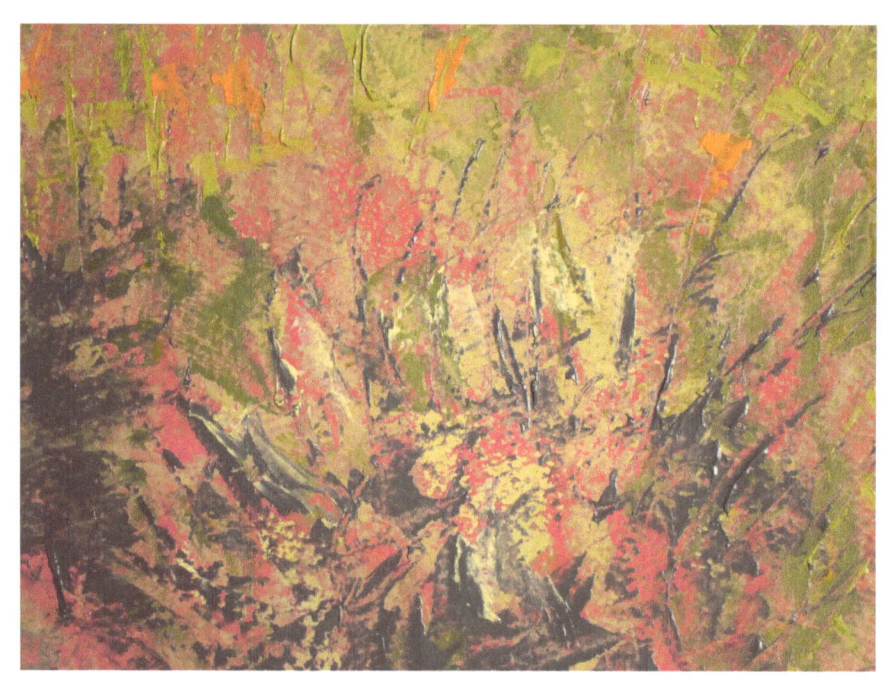

Sanctuary Meadow#1

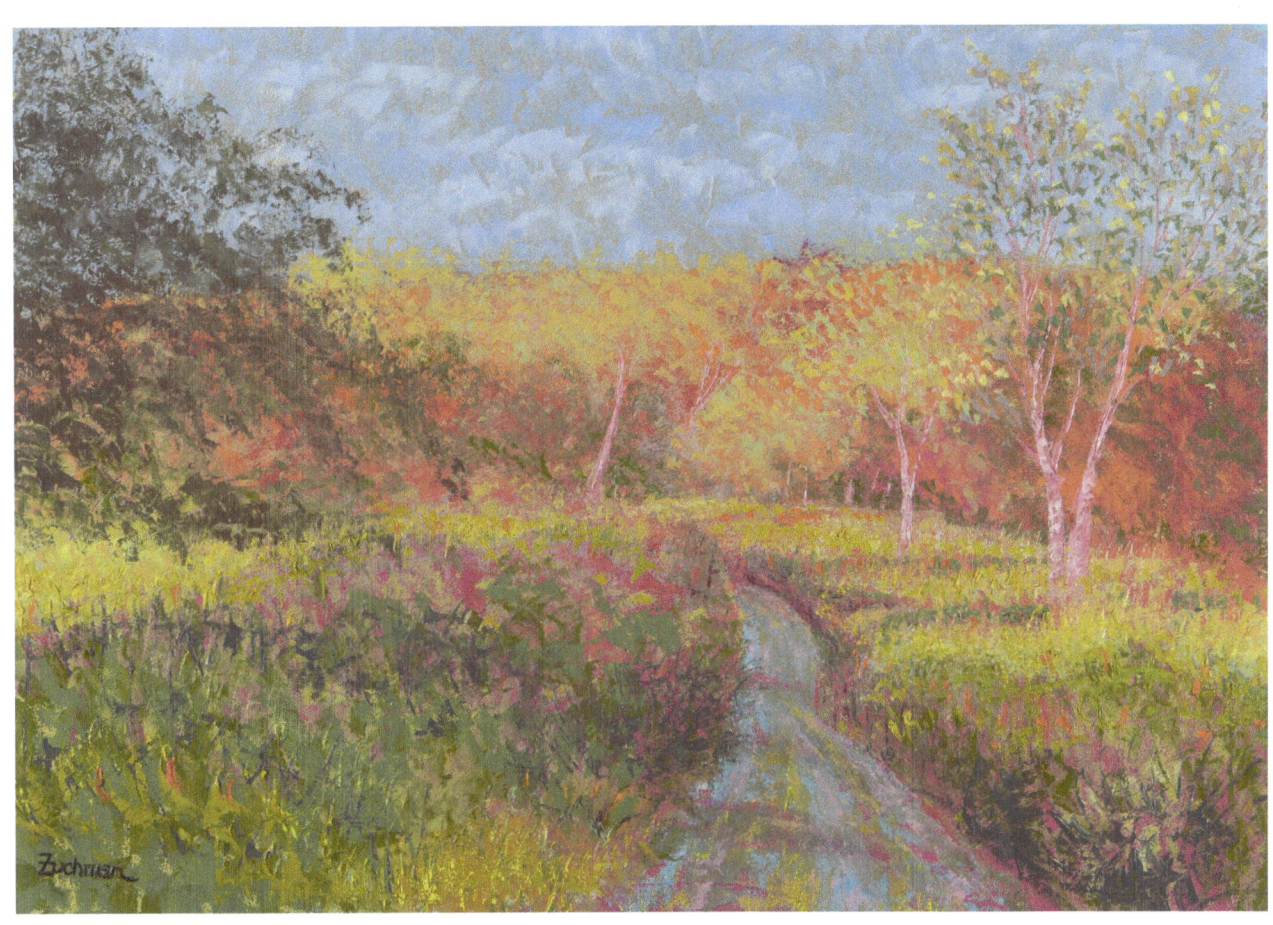

In paint we live with great ambiguity and insights beyond appearances, methods, formulae, convention and logic. To achieve light, we paint darkness; to achieve space, we must achieve flatness; ugliness and discordance can achieve beauty. Those things that work are true.

Apple Orchard at Truesdell's #2

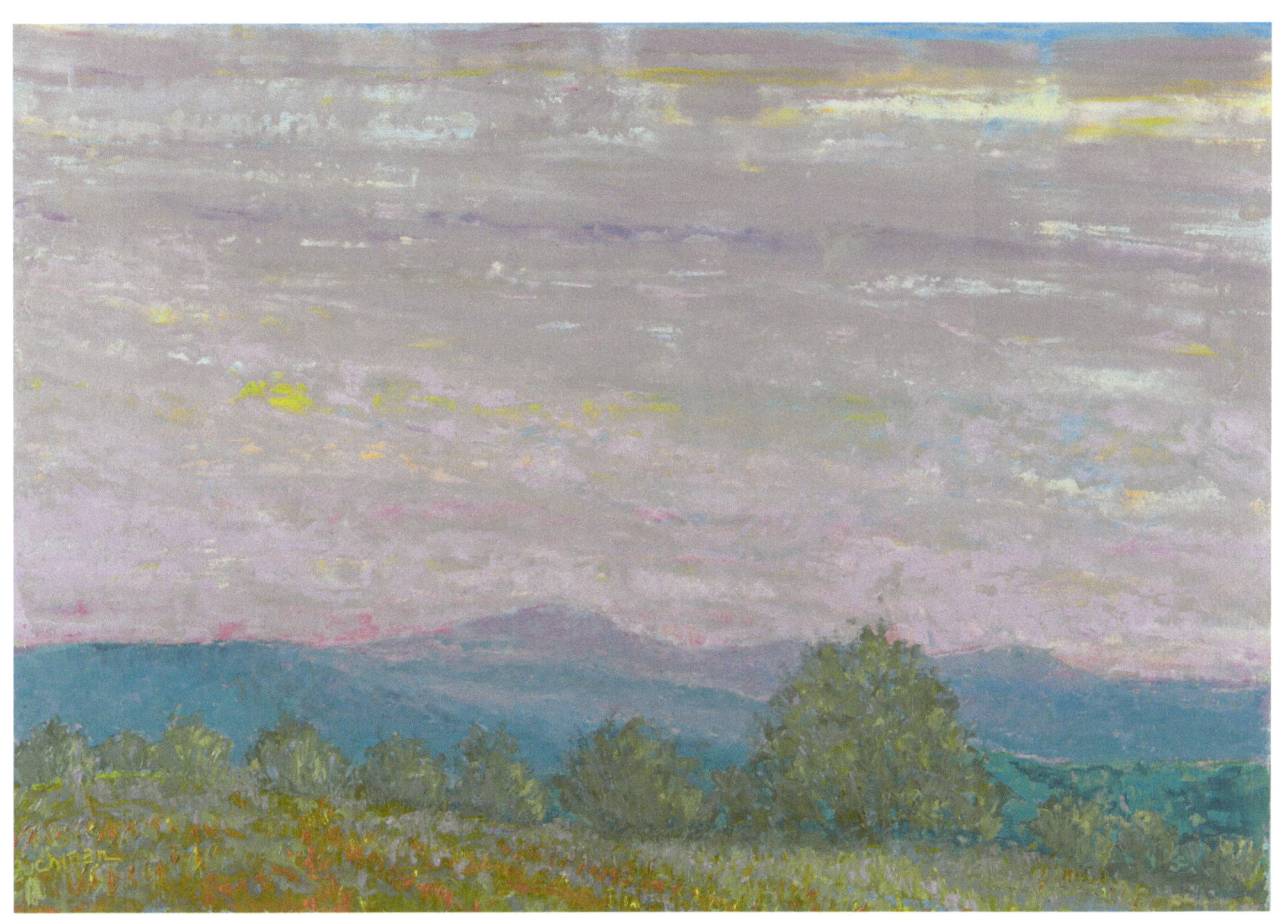

Logging Trail at Little Mohawk

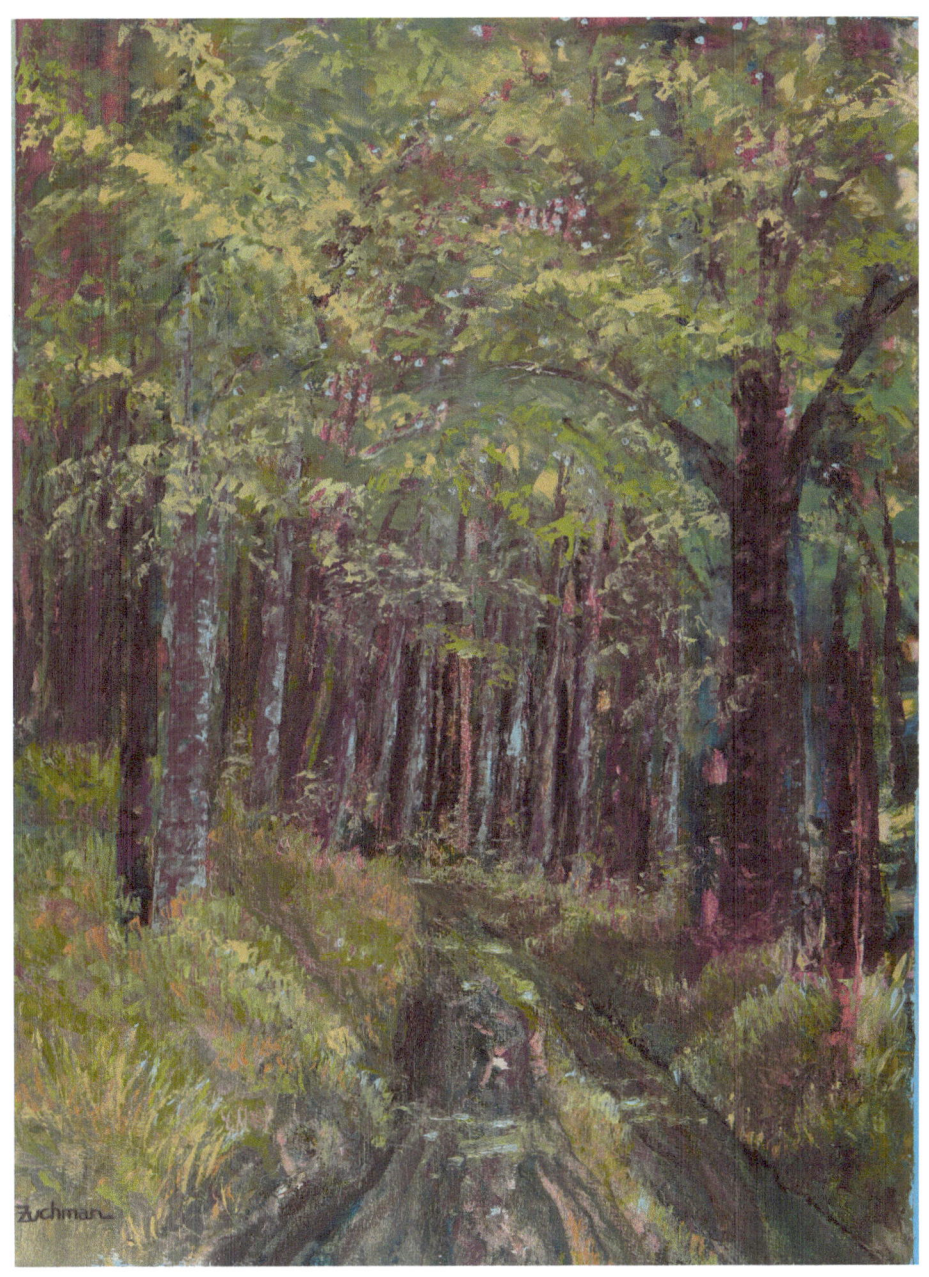

Man is most often absent from my work,
but even wilderness is a reflection of our cultural landscape.
It is not always utopian and idealistic. I do not view the landscape.
I am in it; I am a part of it.

Square Lot Road #1

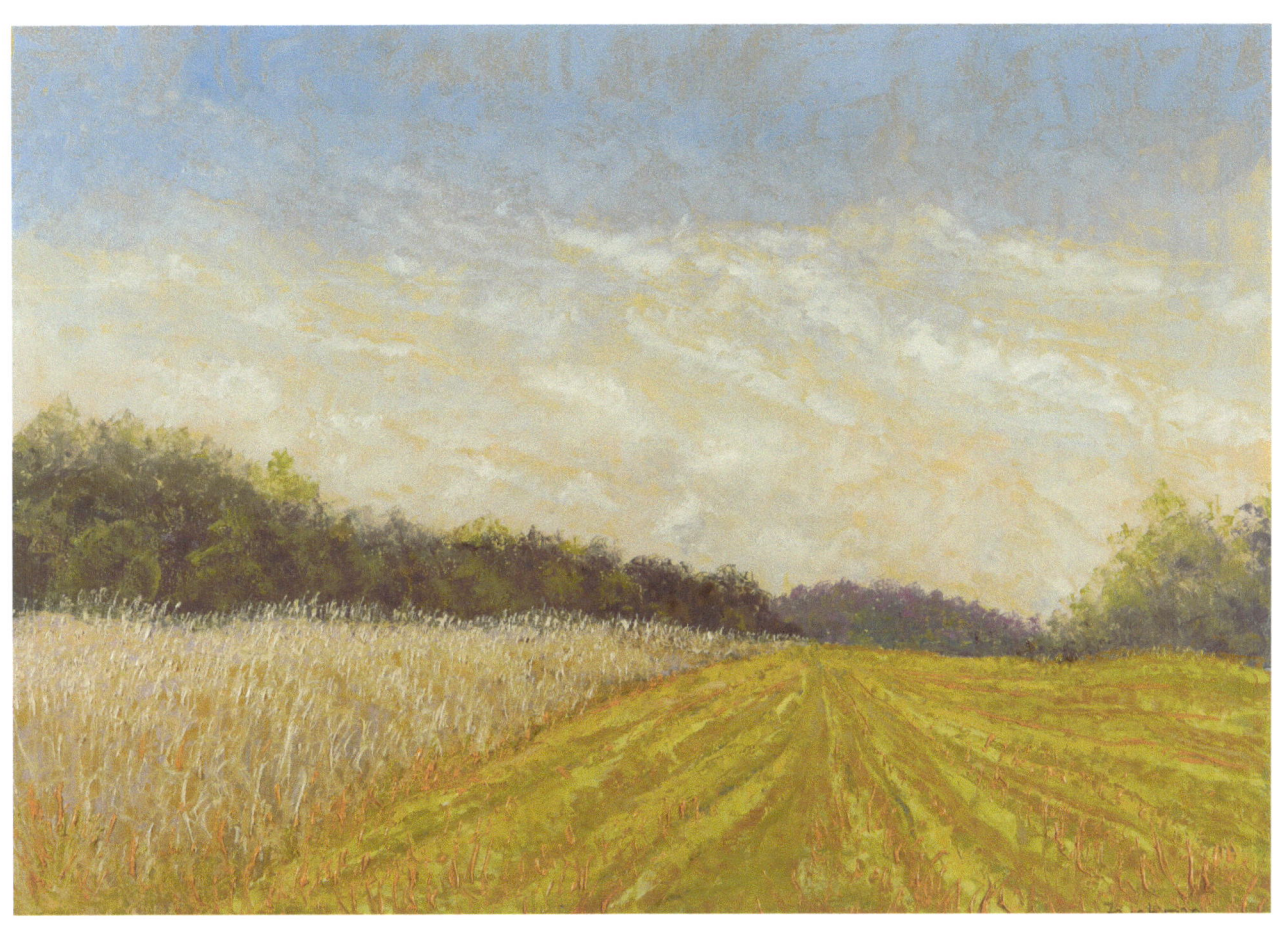

Orcutt Hill, Buckland

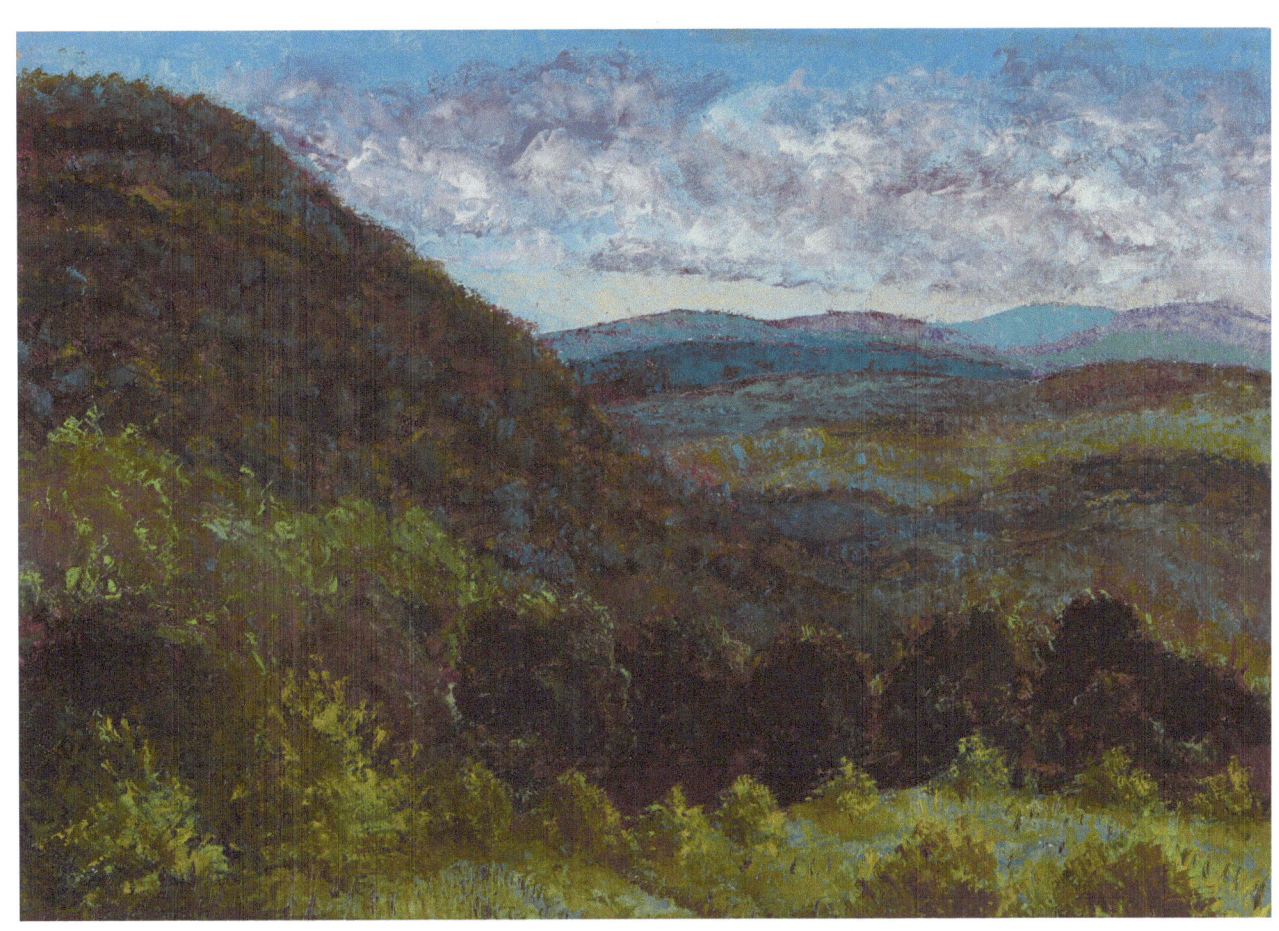

I am not after resemblance, representation or depiction, but more.
I am attempting both the conscious and unconscious presentation,
not a re-presentation.

Swamp at Goldswaithe's #3

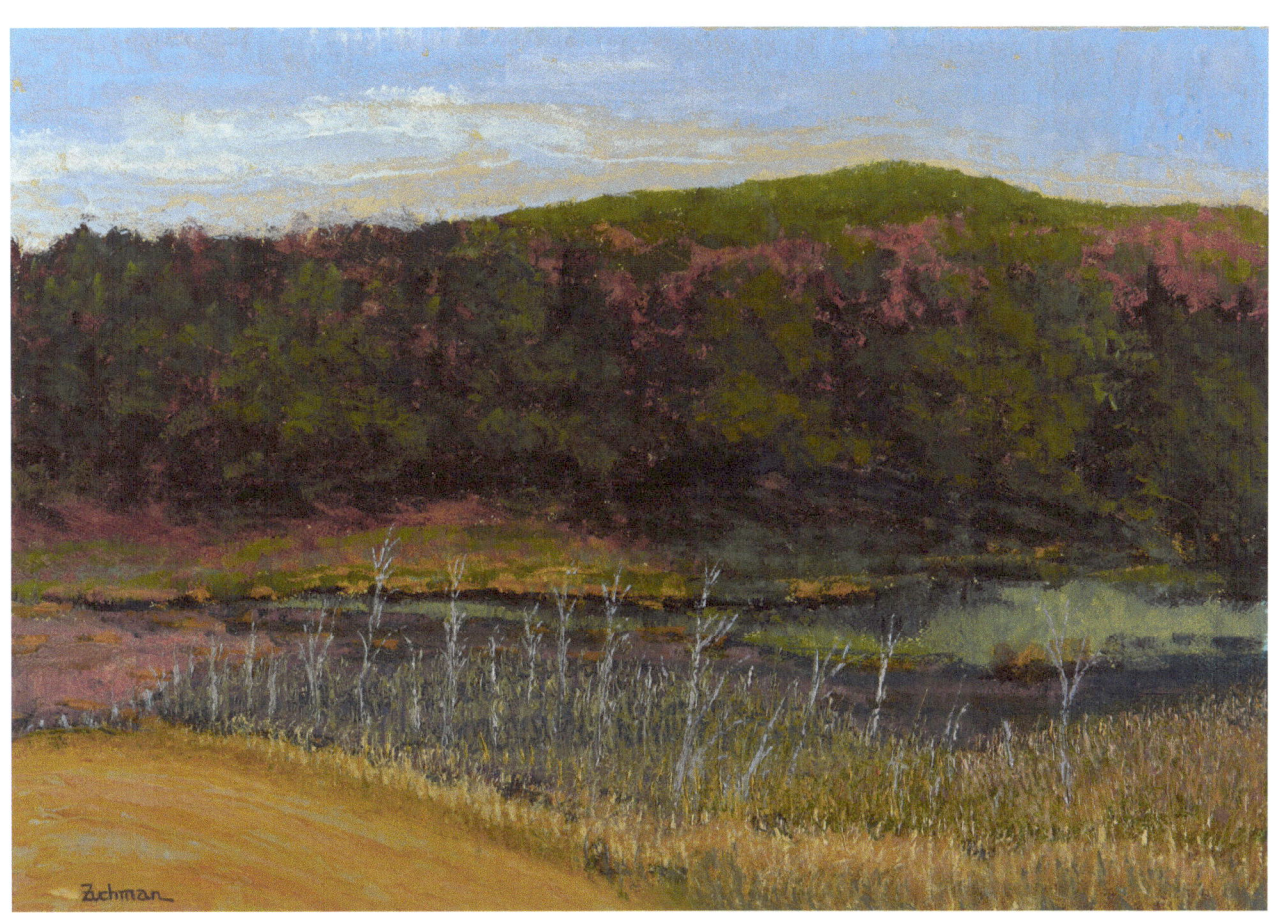

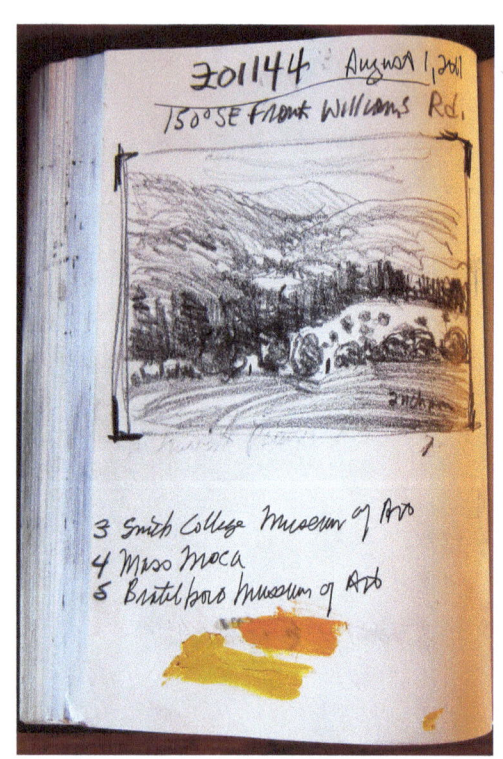

From Frank Williams Road

44

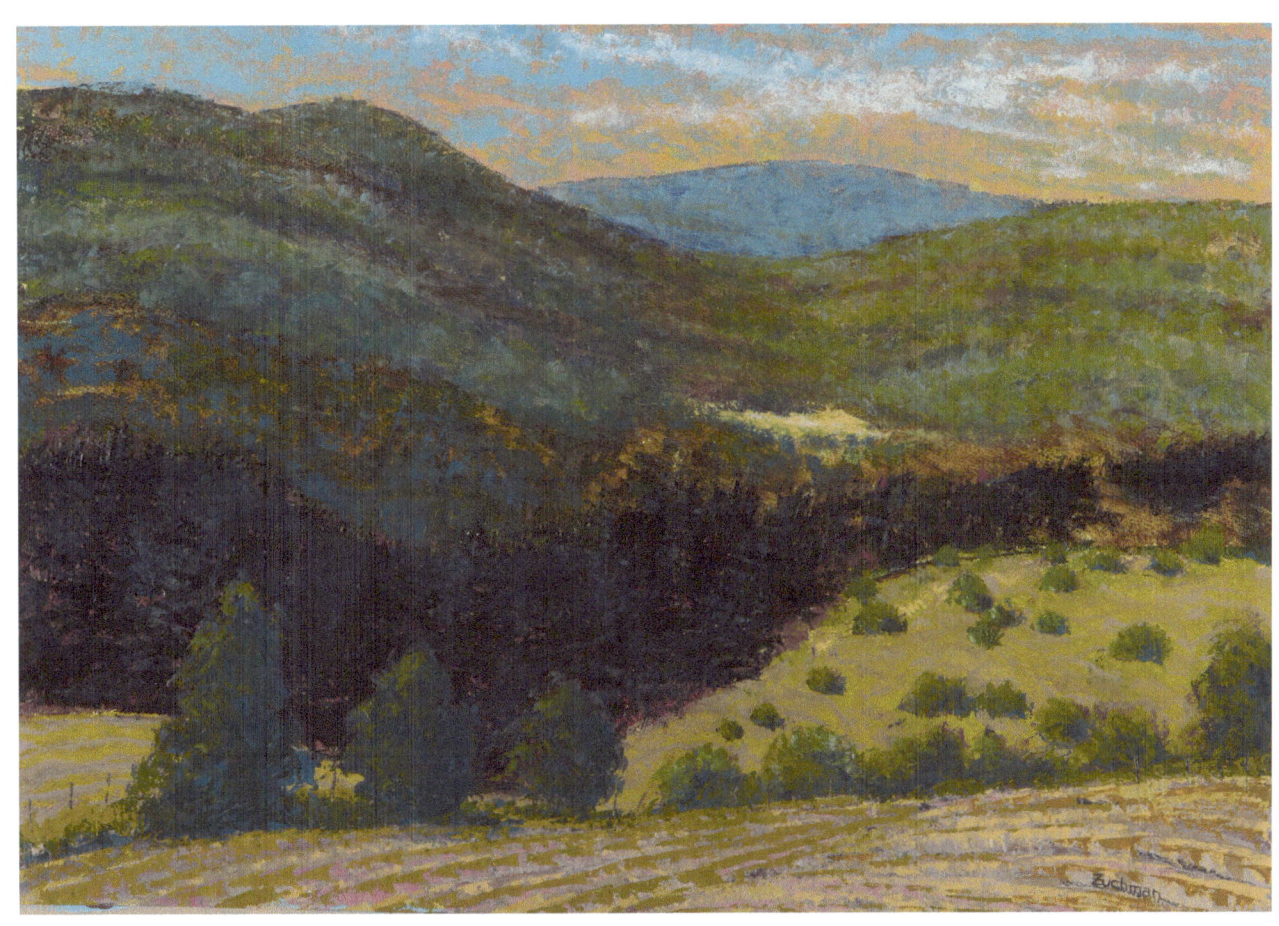

Lower Lot at Frankton Road

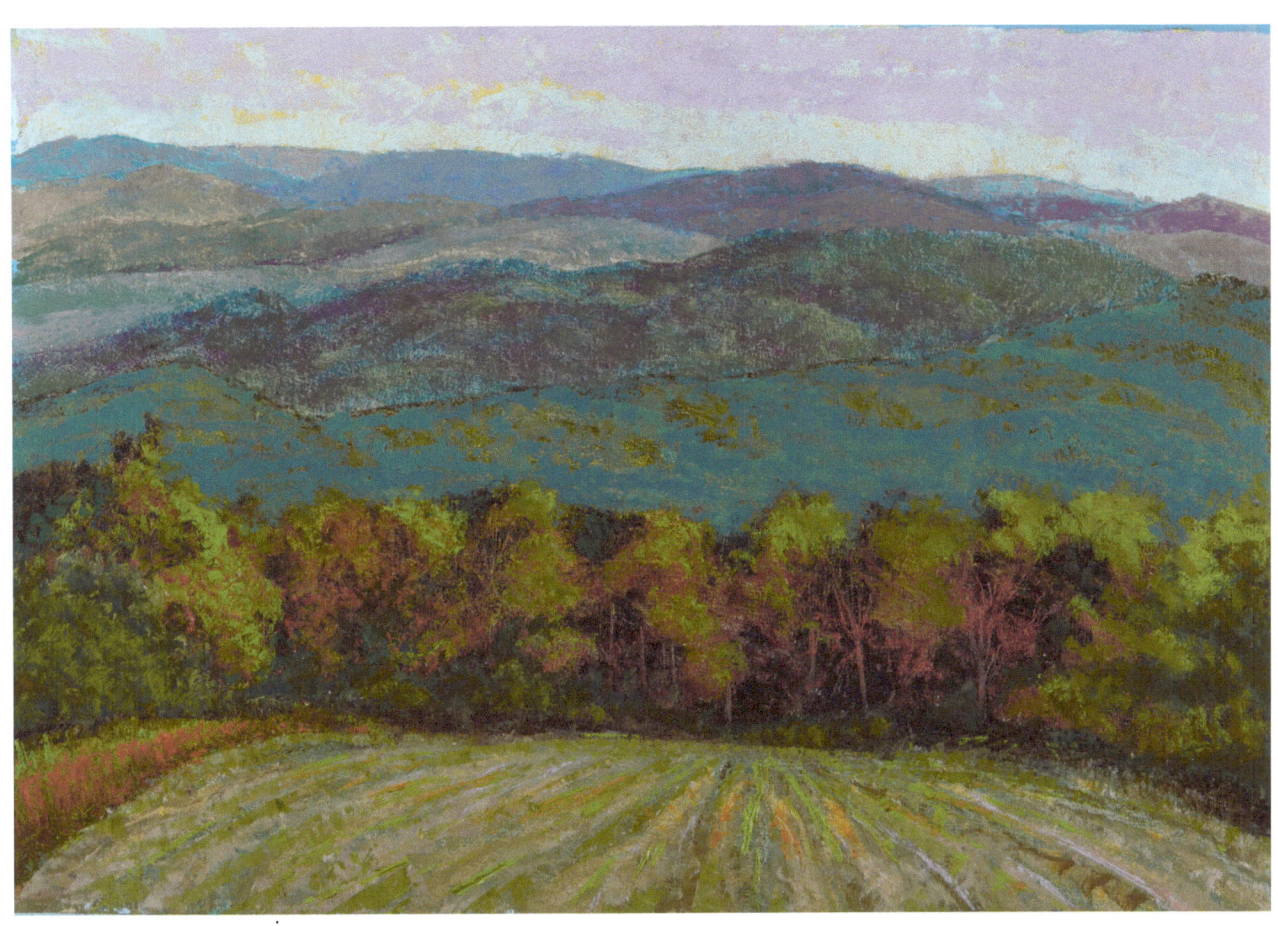

Exposing the Spirit

Correspondences, seen through the eye alone,
Though trained through the arm,
Not enough.
The image goes through another lens,
That of spirit;
Pulled this way and that,
Twisted, righted, negated,
Fixed, reaffirmed,
That makes art.

Raking at Turkey Trees

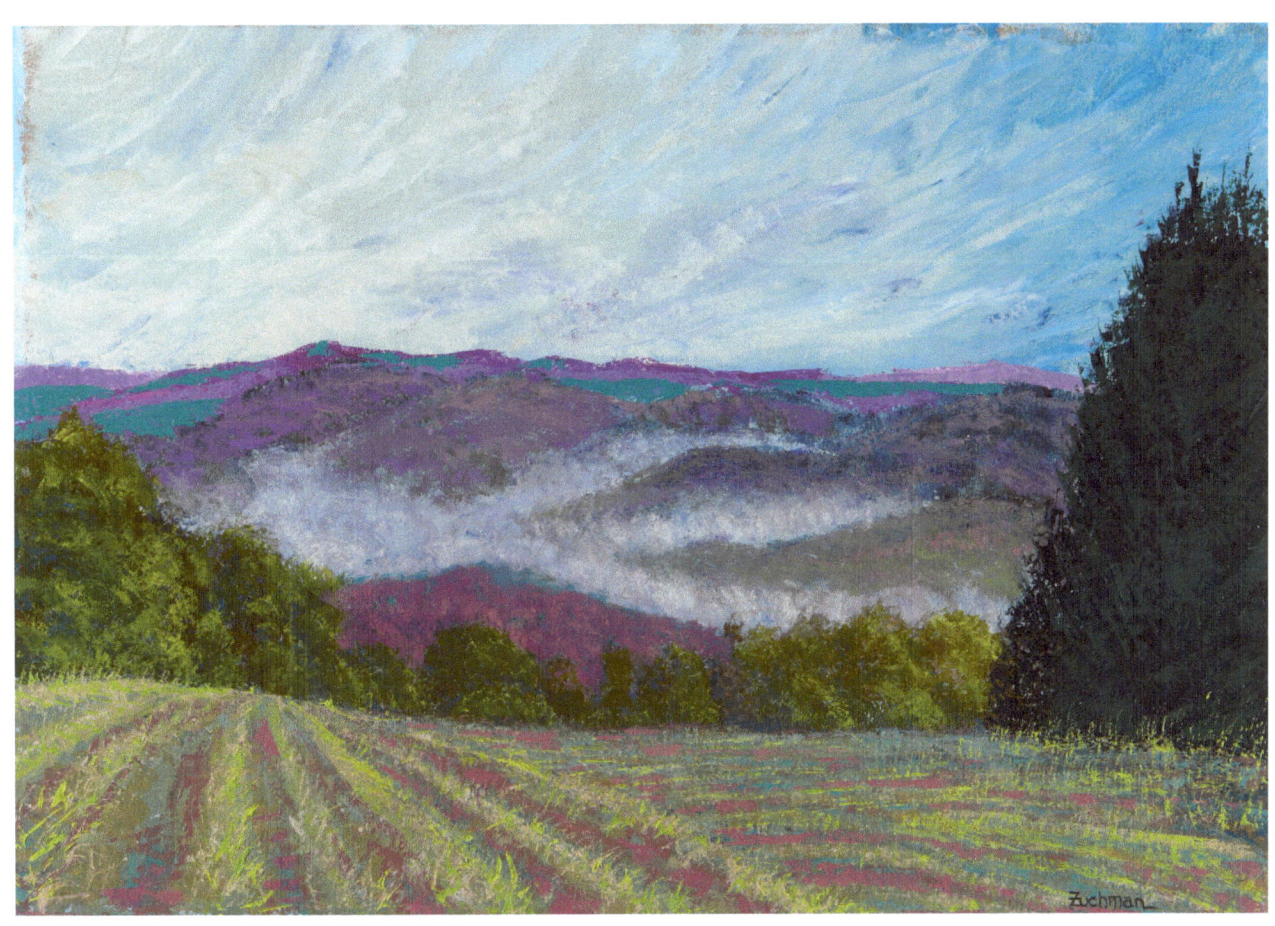

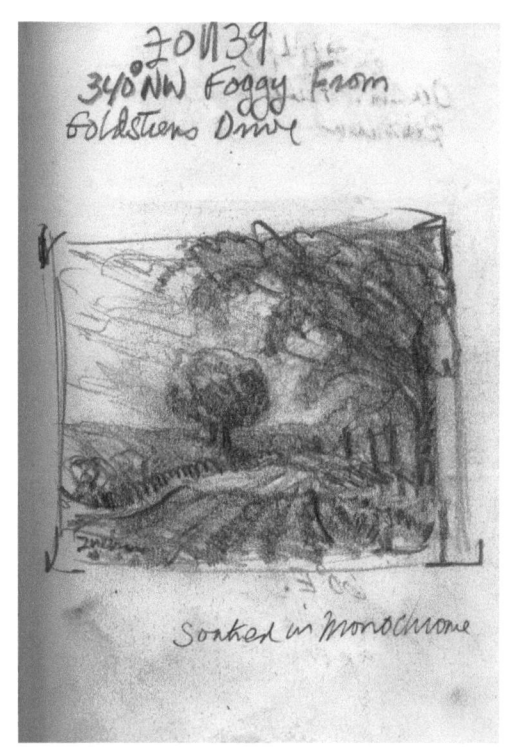

Soaked in Monochrome

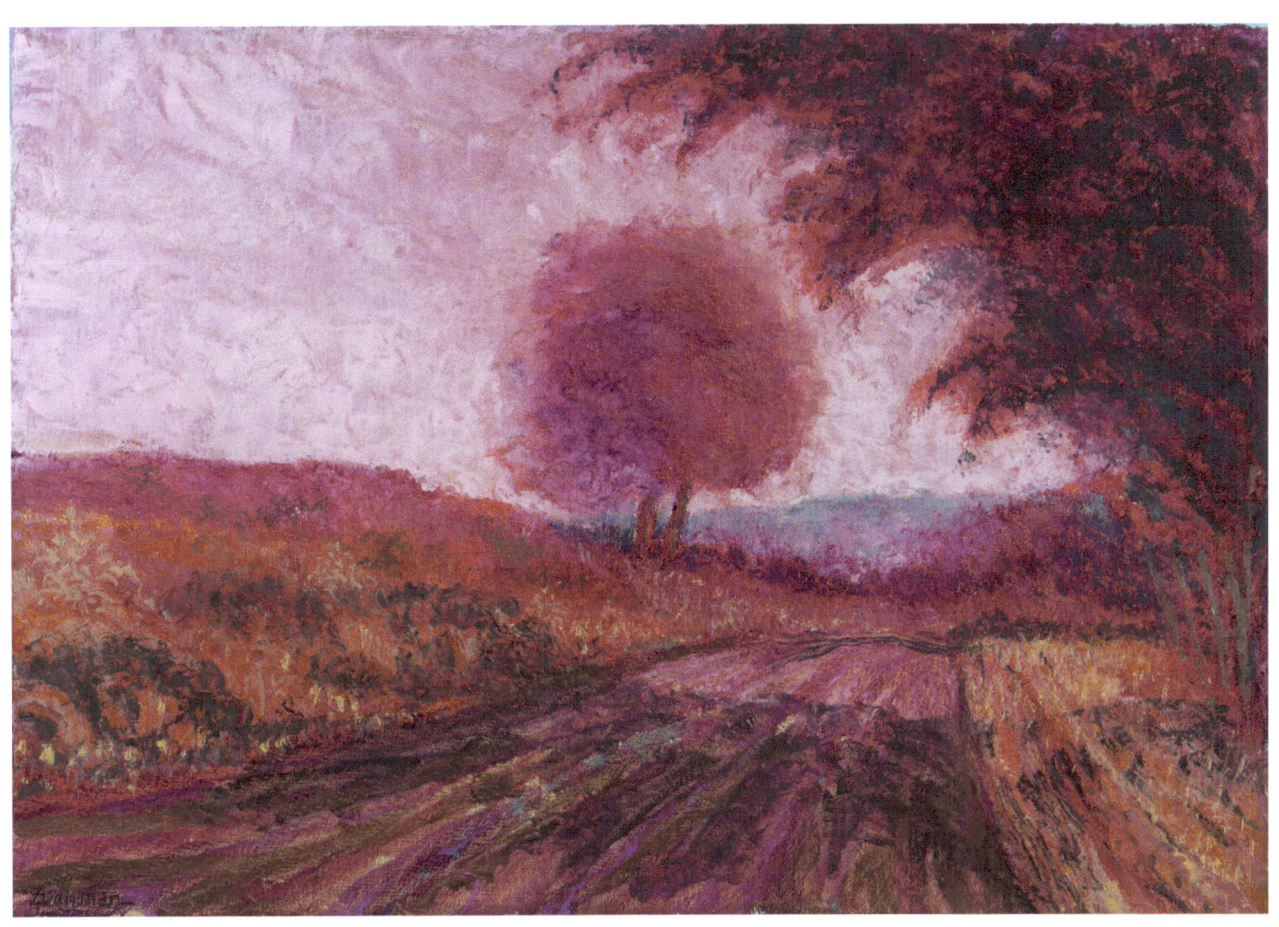

51

Landscape is a relational art which positions man
in a cosmological order, imbeds him.
The landscape viewer is particularly important because this form
demands that we revision ourselves, not as the center of the universe,
not as separate, or subordinate, but as inhabitants of nature.

Wheeler Farm

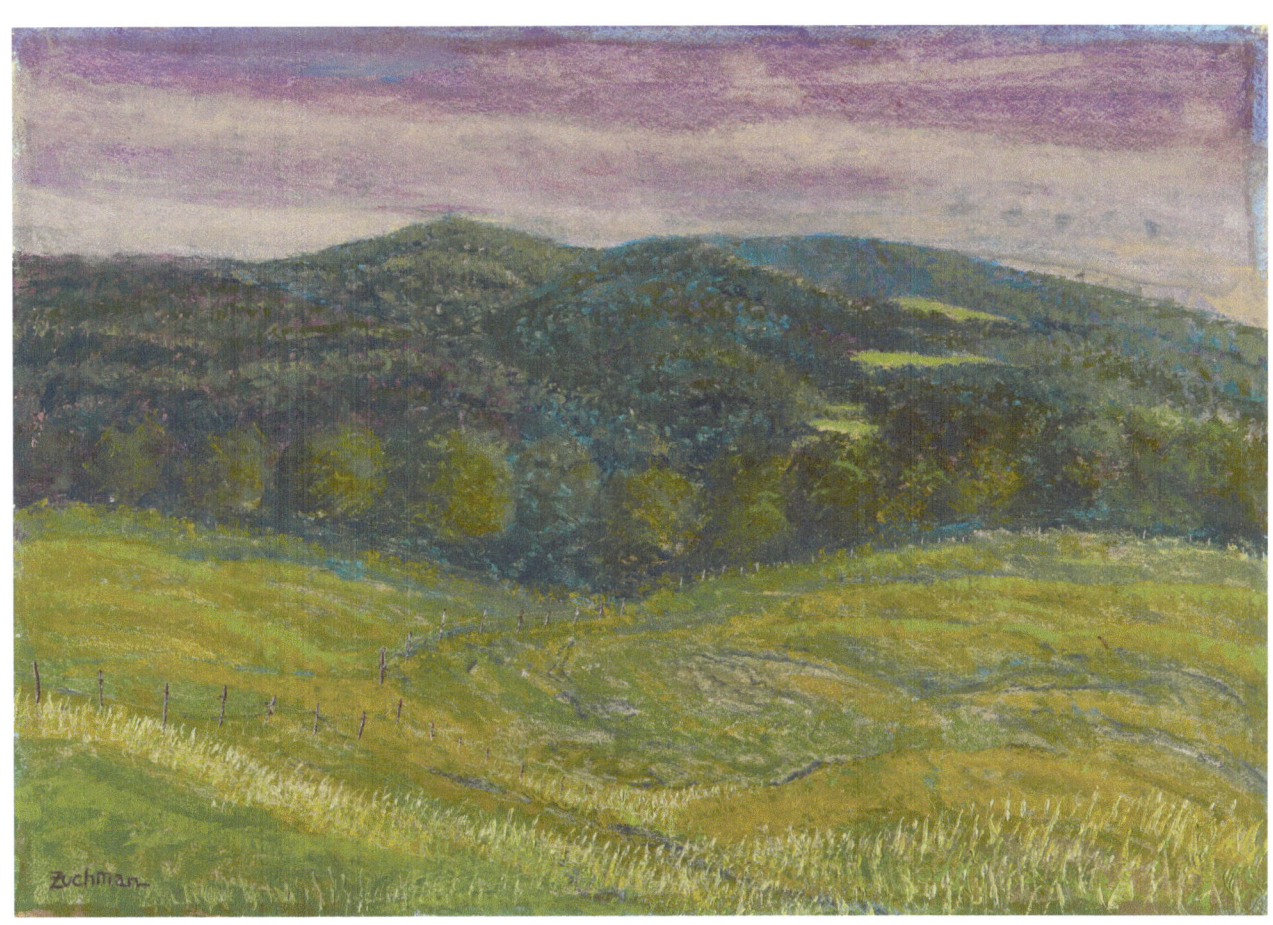

High Ledges in Fog

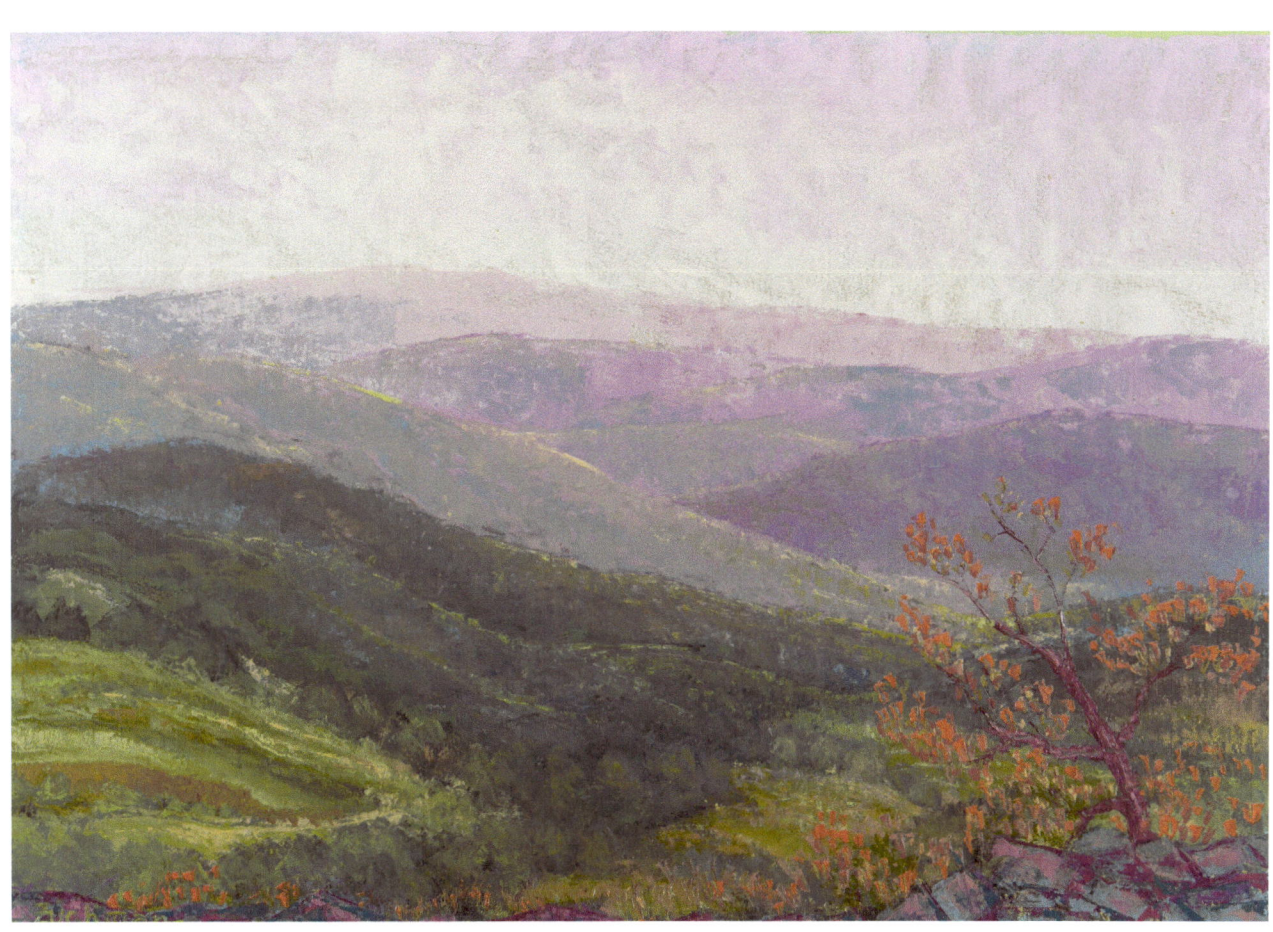

*In many ways the landscape contains political, social,
psychological, historical and spiritual content.
The fence, the wall, the gate, the field, the path, the road,
the house are not quite symbols but re-presentations of autonomy
and order in which are written the history of mankind.*

East From Washer's

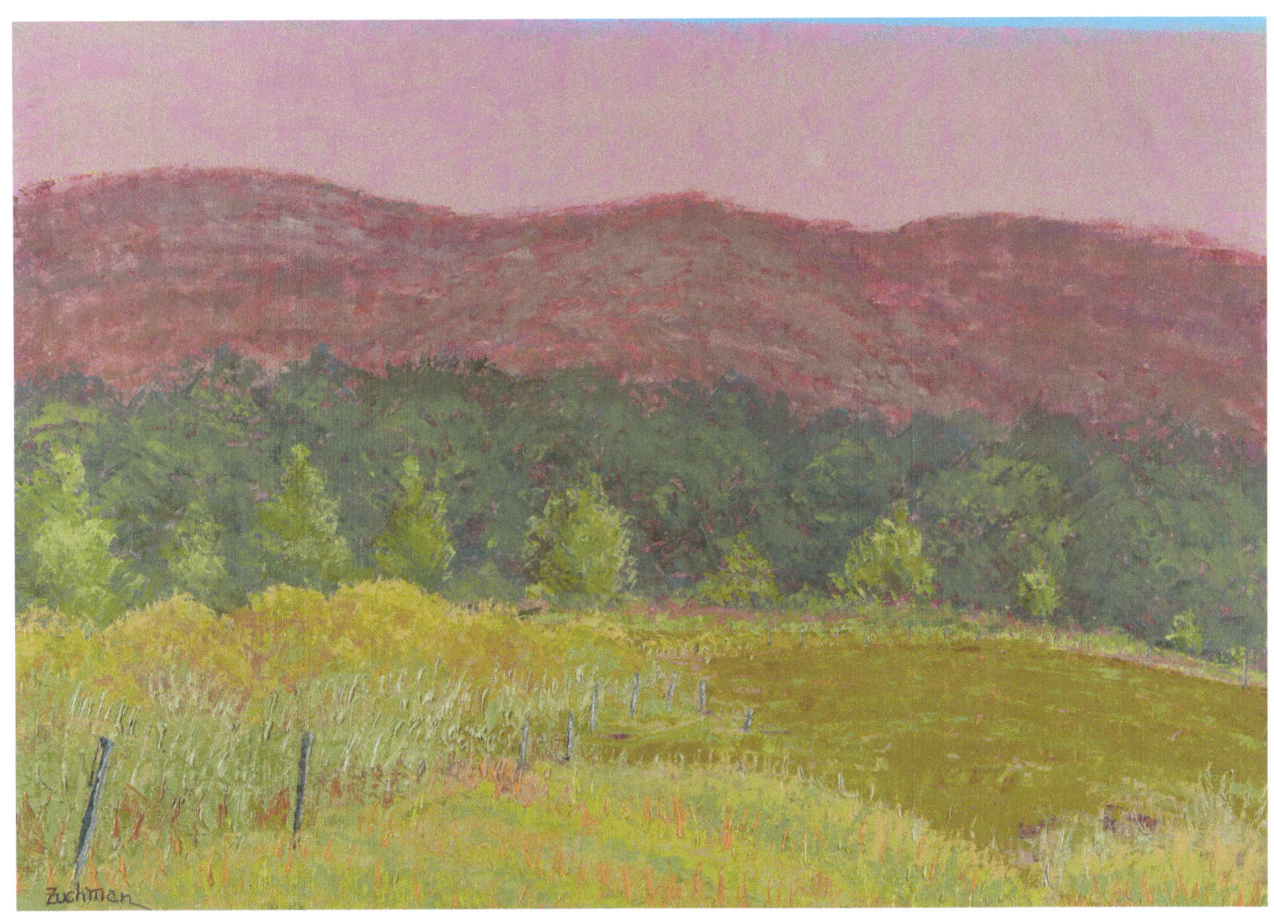

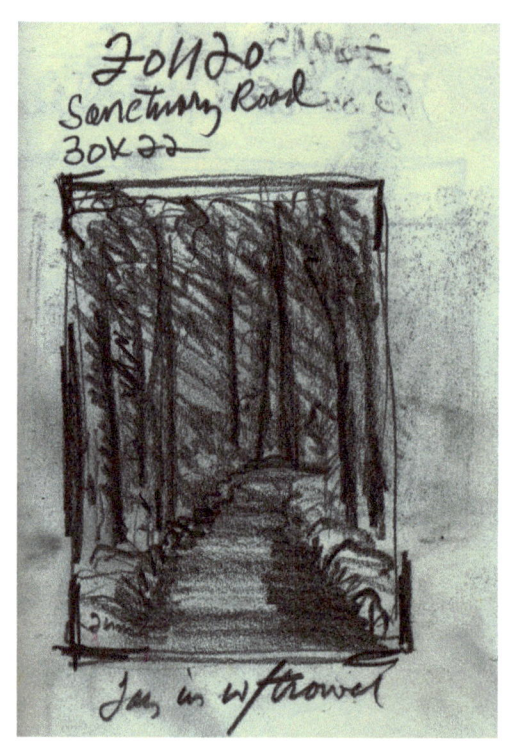

Sanctuary Road

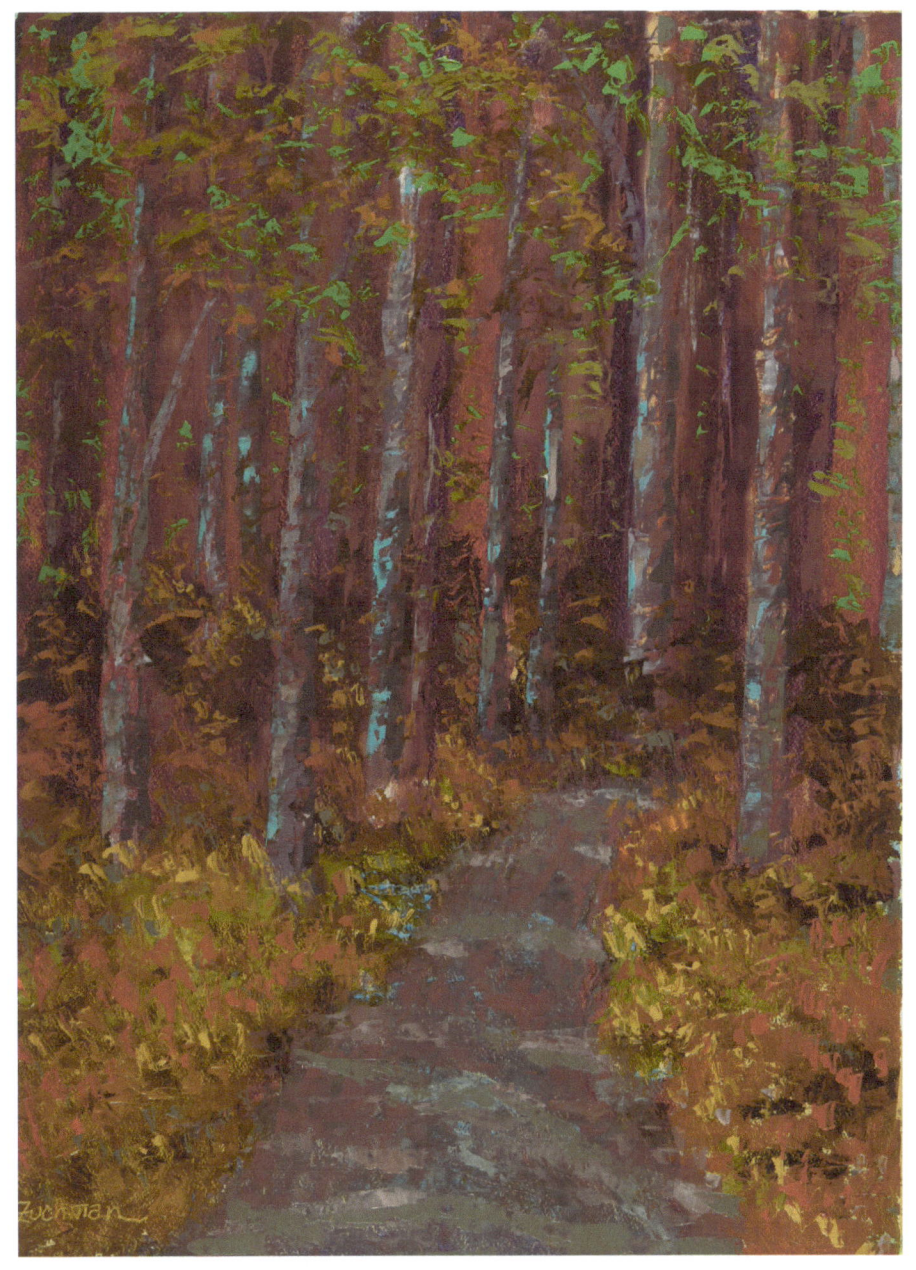

Turkey Trees #1

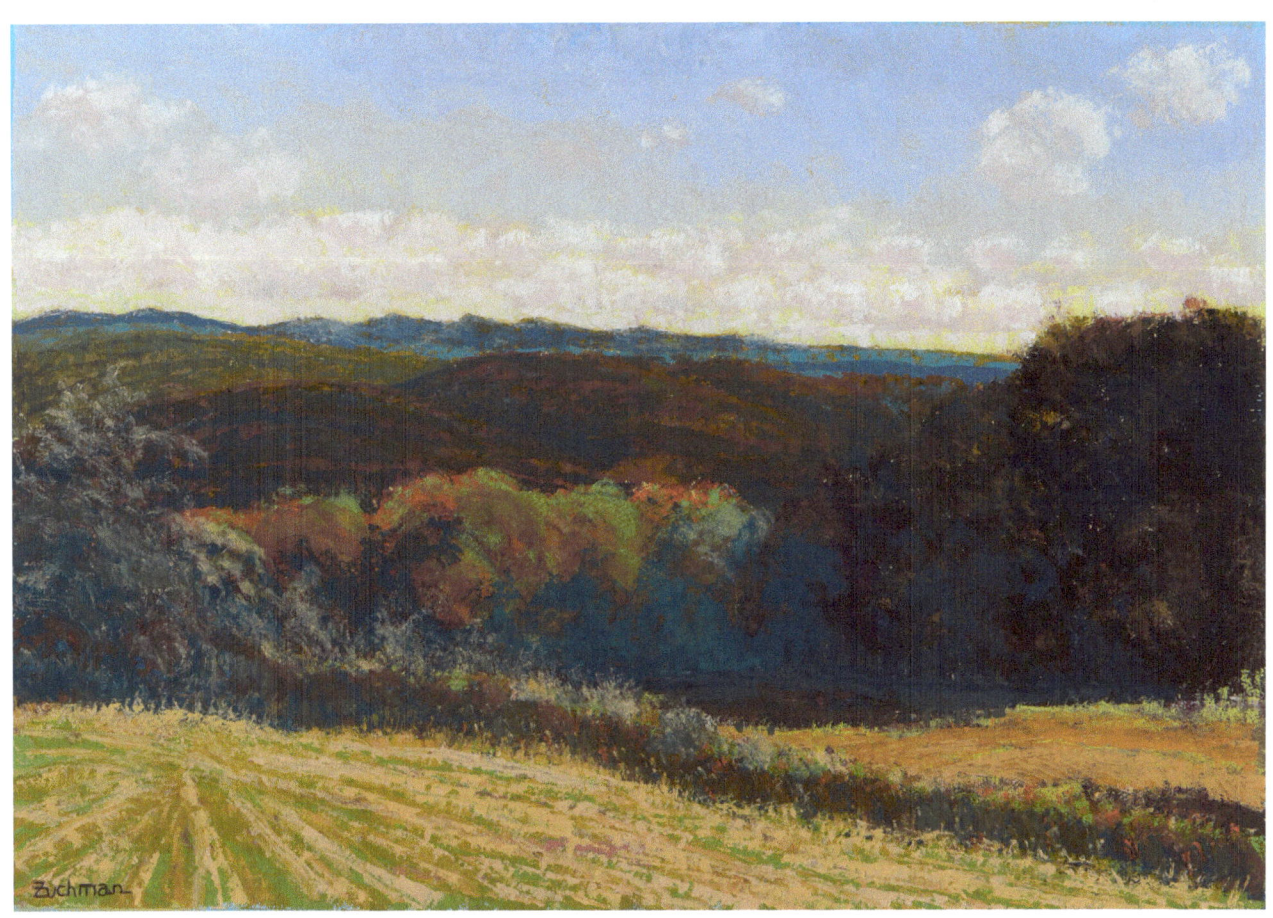

In the landscape, man can look down and soar with transcendence or look up with humbling finiteness. The landscape offers stepping stones into dream formation, contemplation and metaphysical thought.

Goldswaithe's South #1

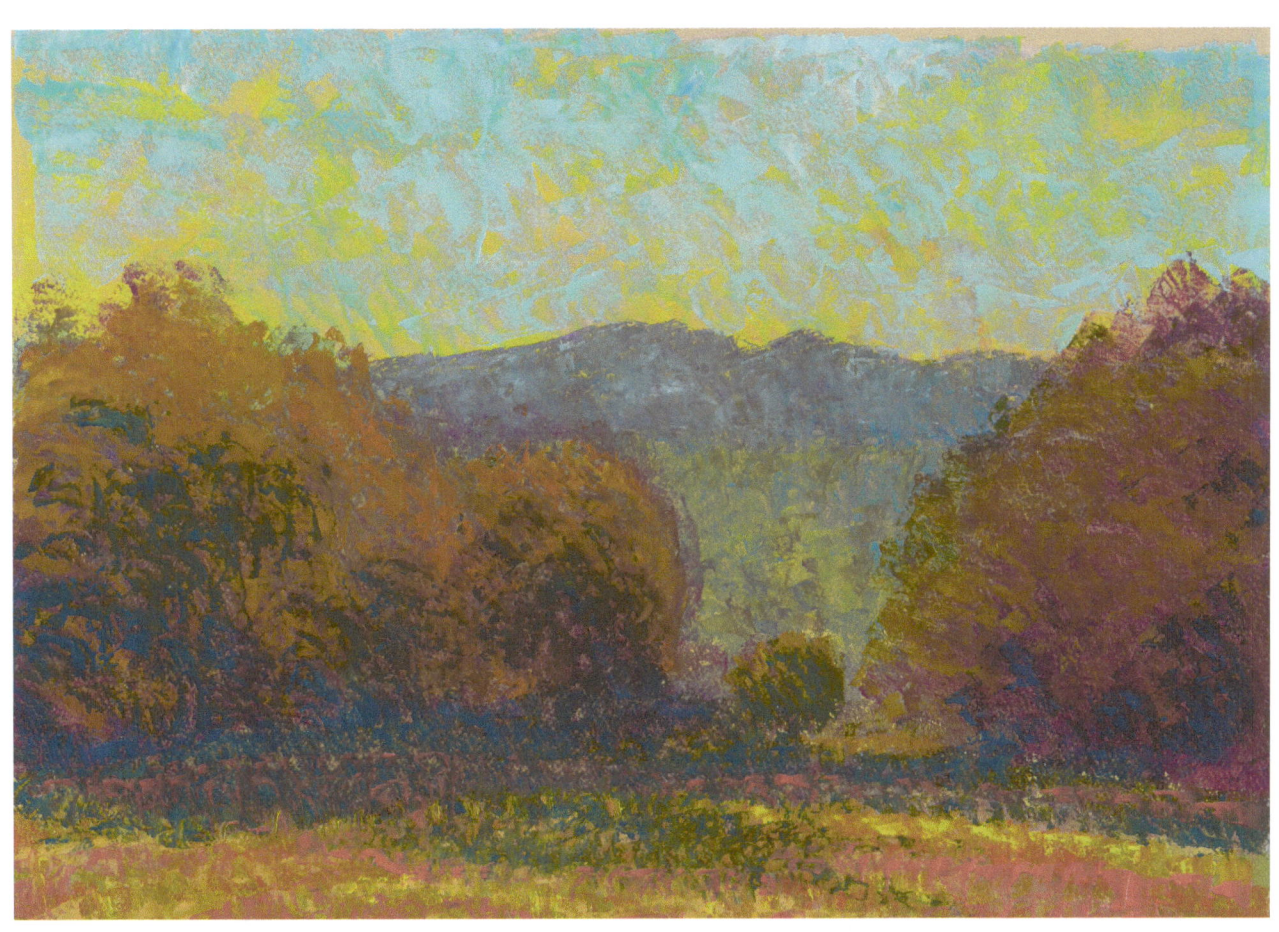

Goldswaithe's South #2

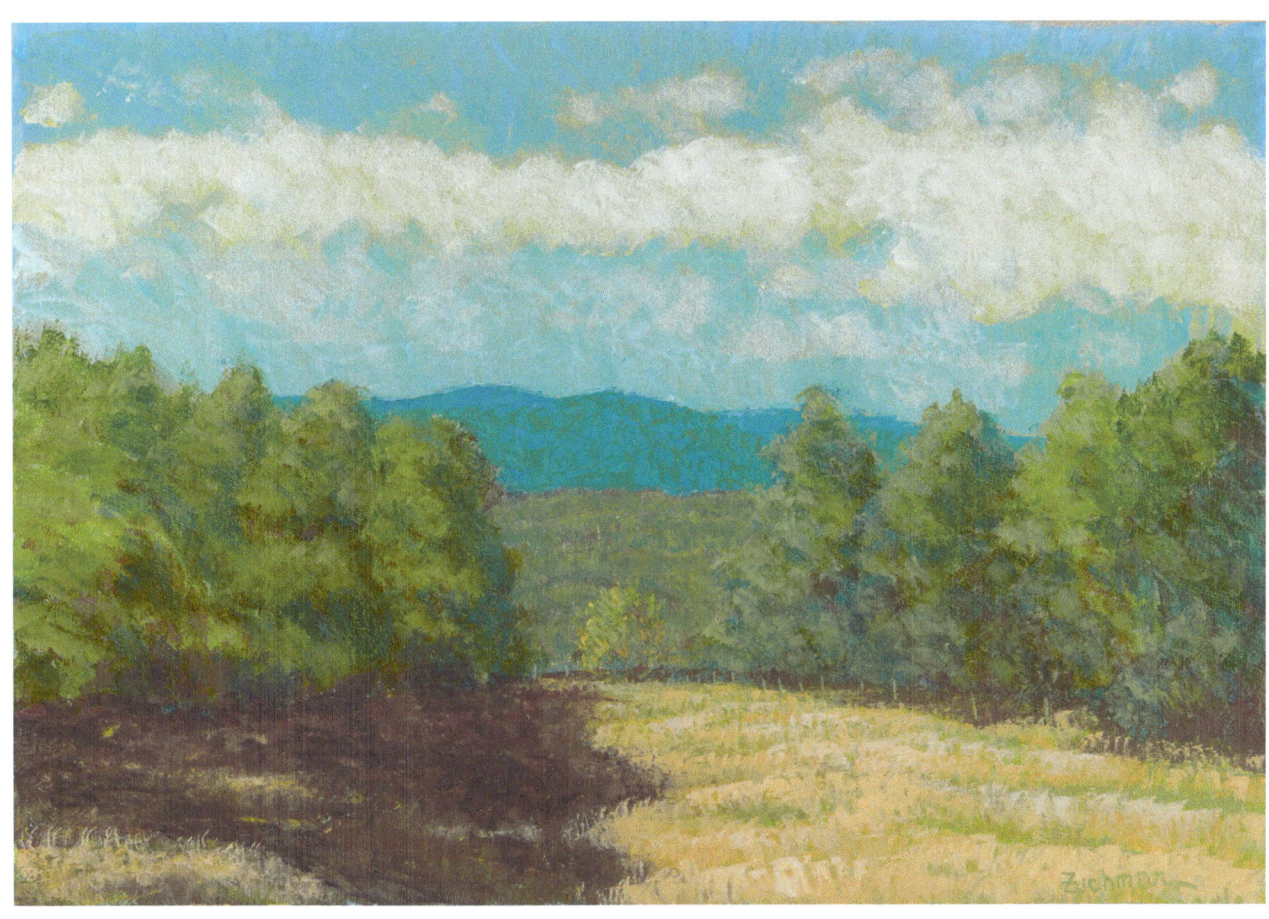

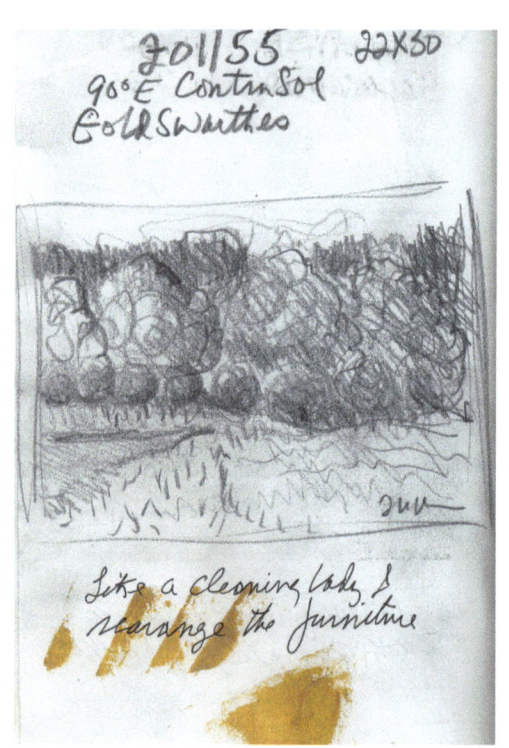

Like a cleaning lady &
rearange the furniture

Contra Sol

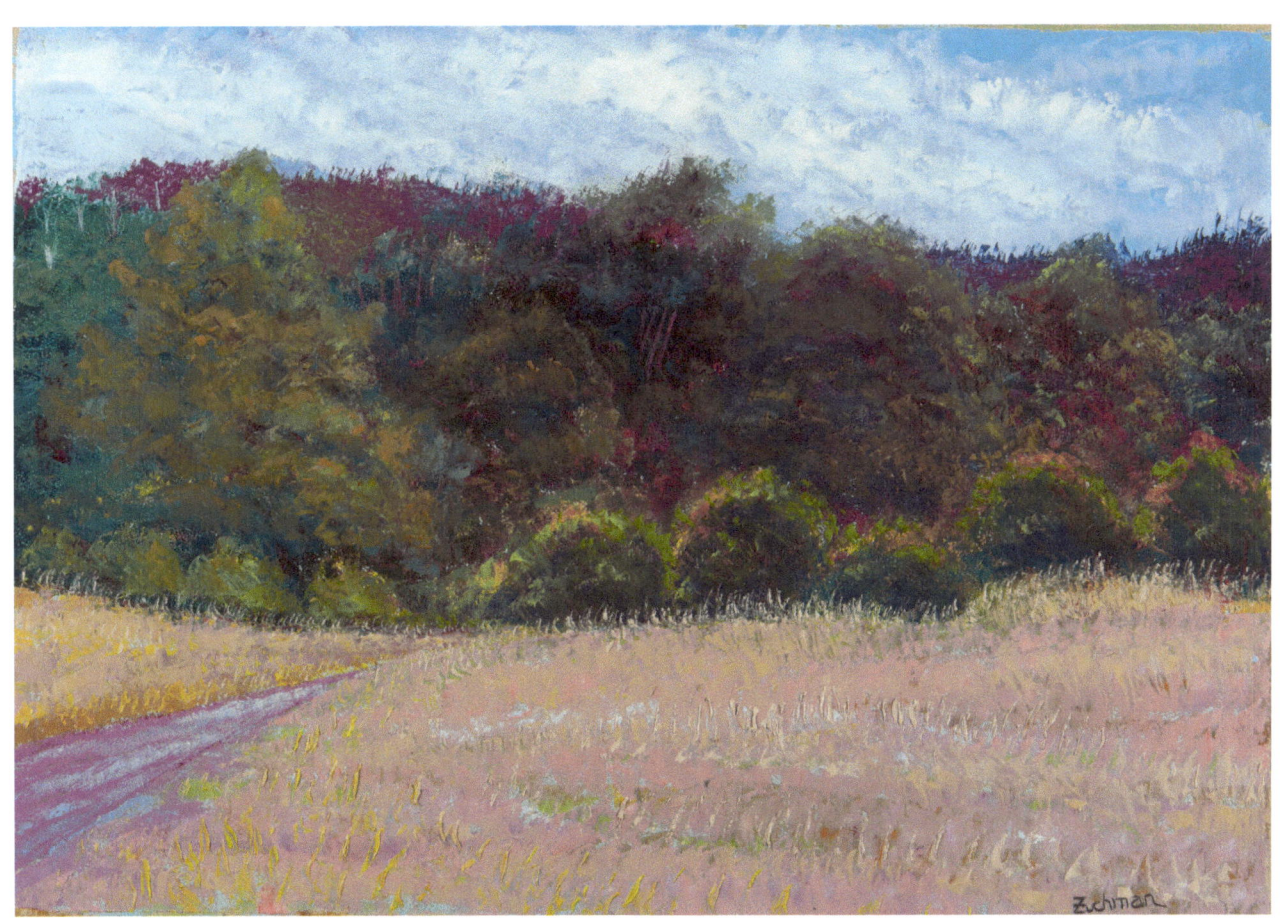

Square Lot Road #2

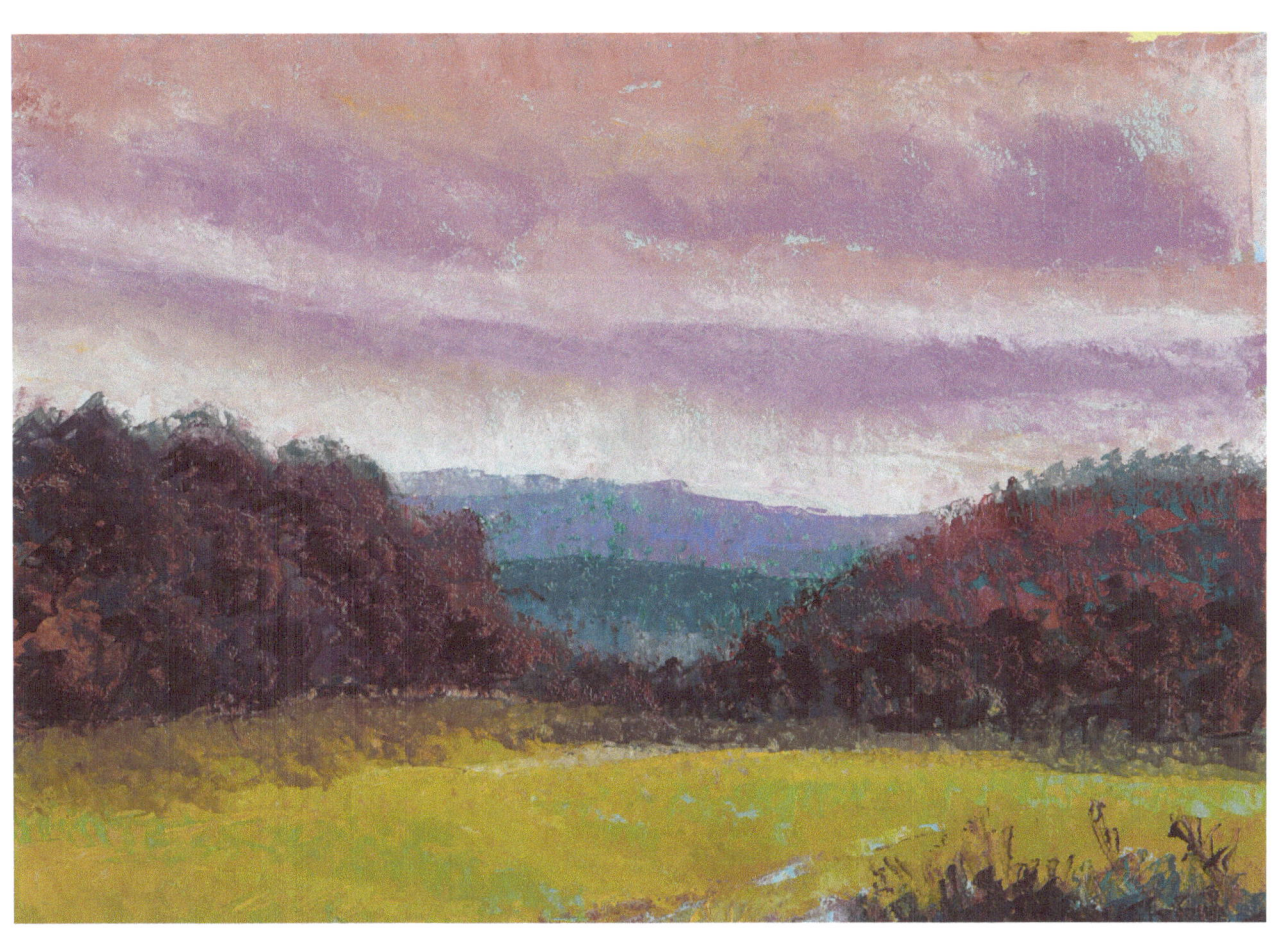

The artist's location, or point of view, sets the tone for the viewer's relationship to the landscape. A low horizon elevates the viewer and creates transcendence; a high horizon makes the viewer humble. Here the artist works out the problem of man and space and man and his place.

Sanctuary Meadow #3

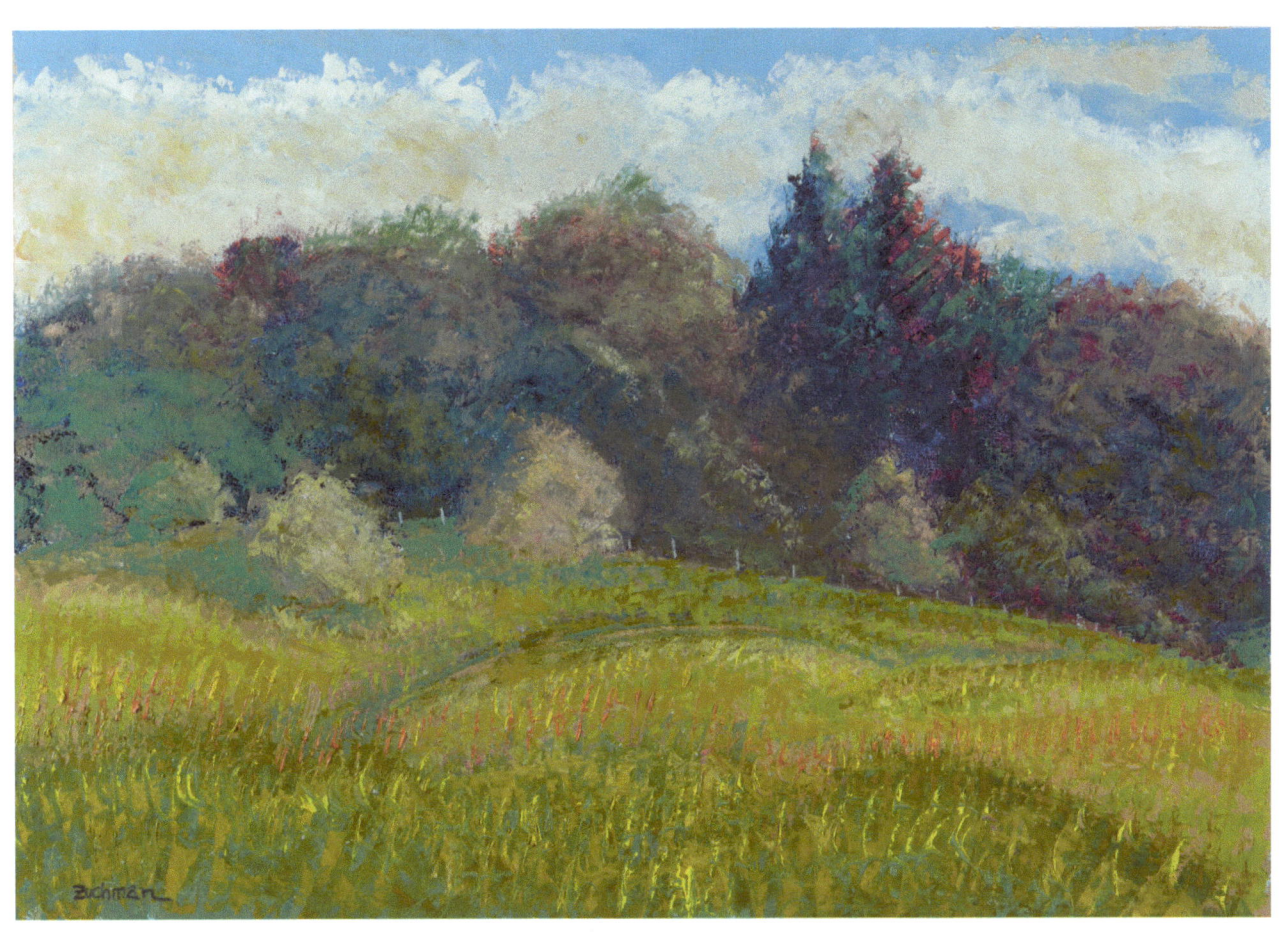

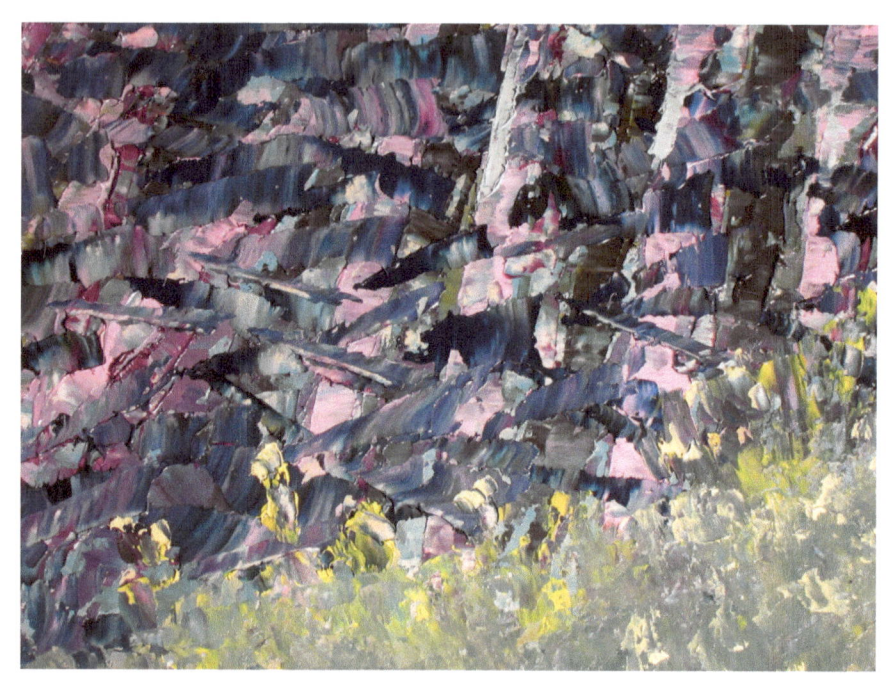

Sunrise, Colrain Watershed

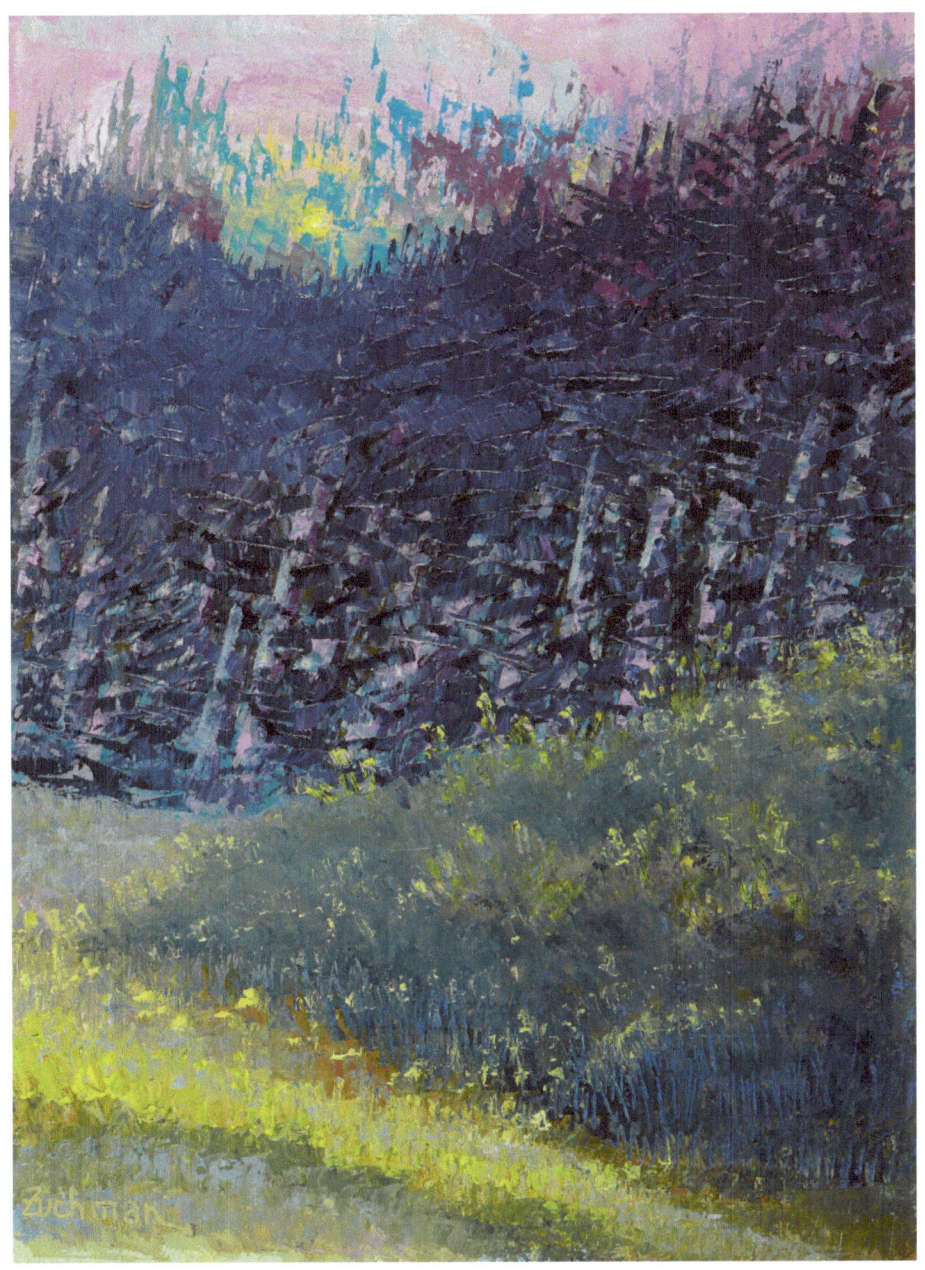

Turkey Trees #2

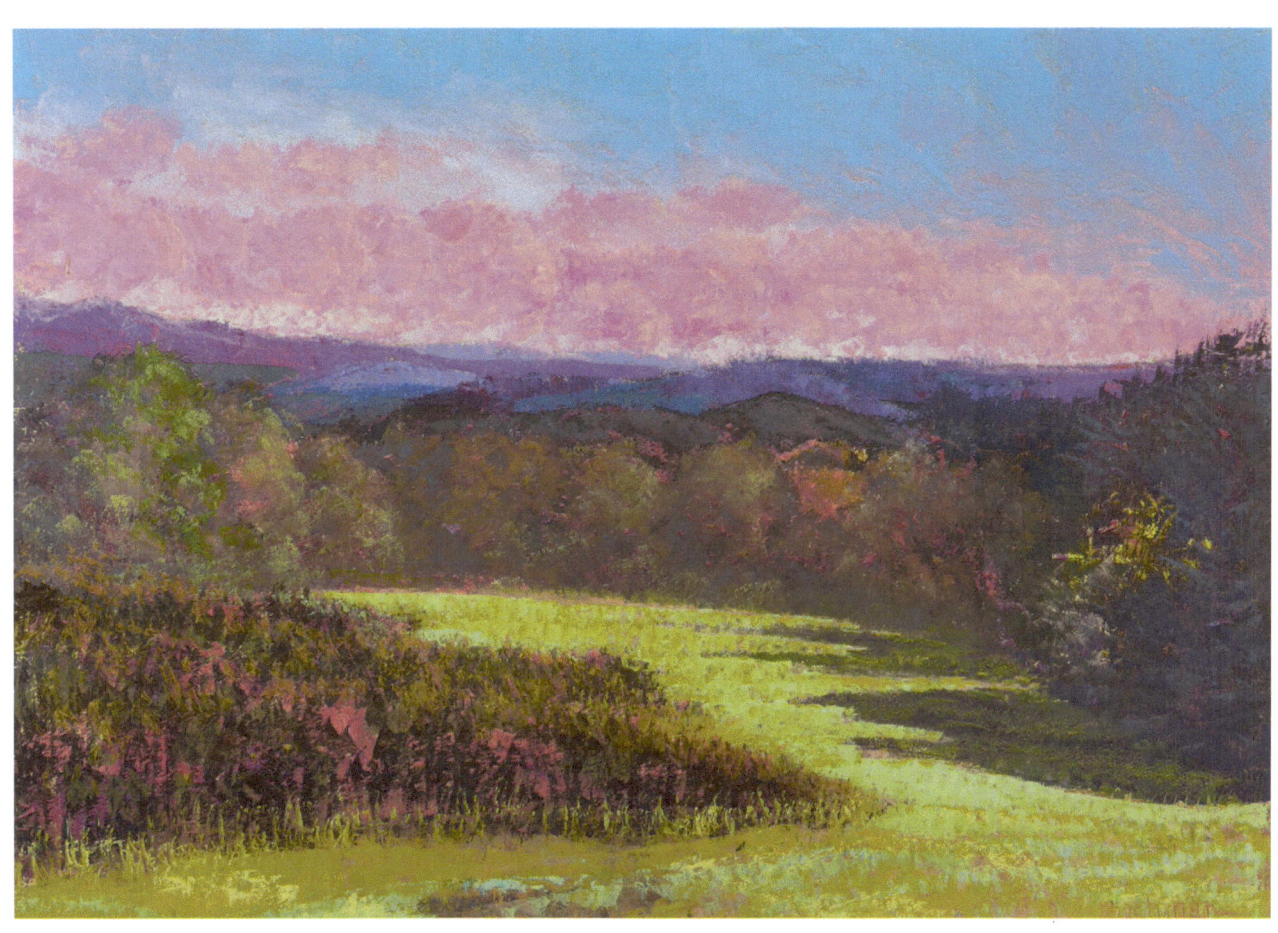

Landscape painting includes the whole of nature,
including man, and makes a case for us, too.
Its importance now cannot be underestimated.

Topped Trees, Colrain Watershed

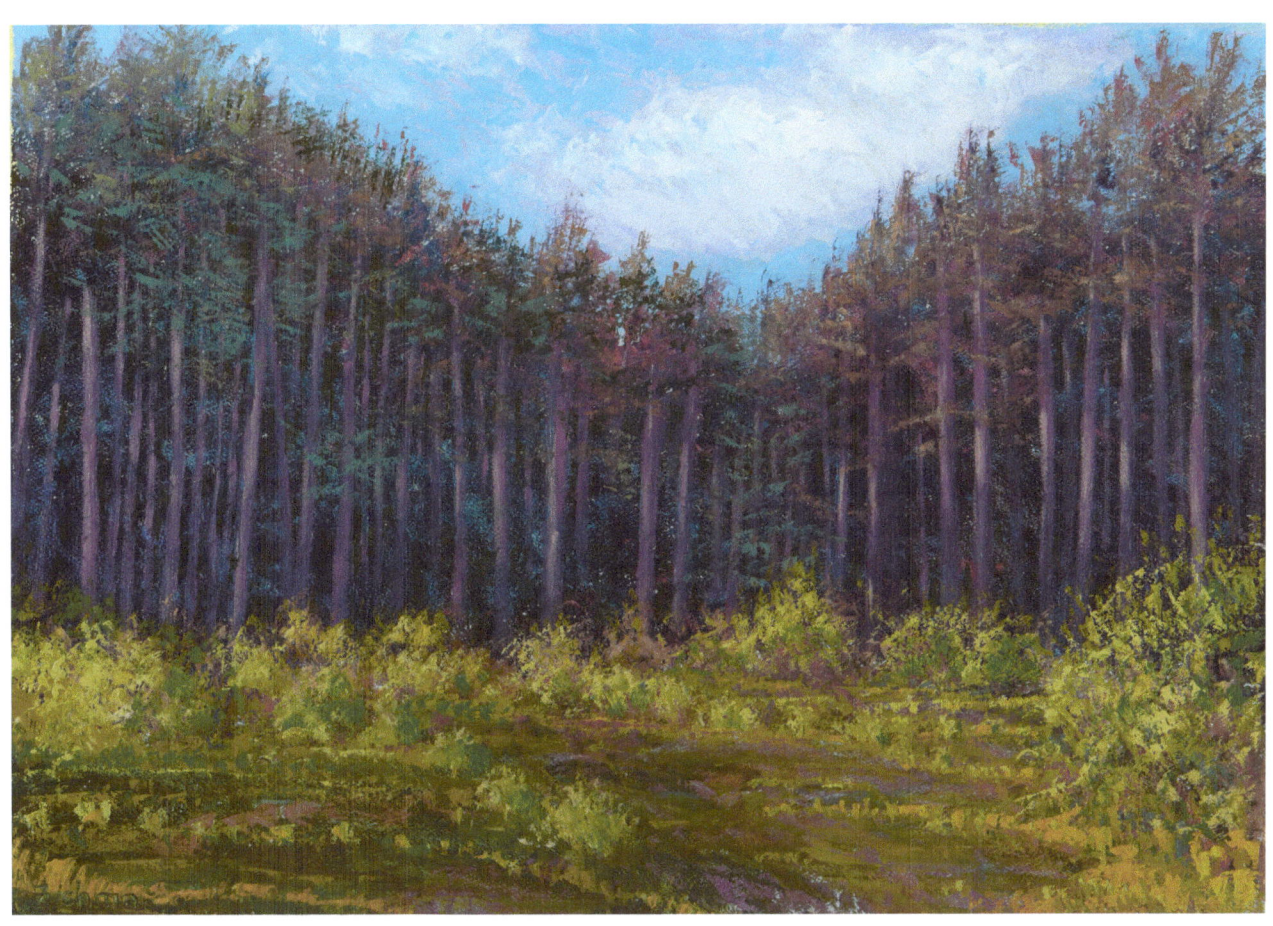

The Rocks

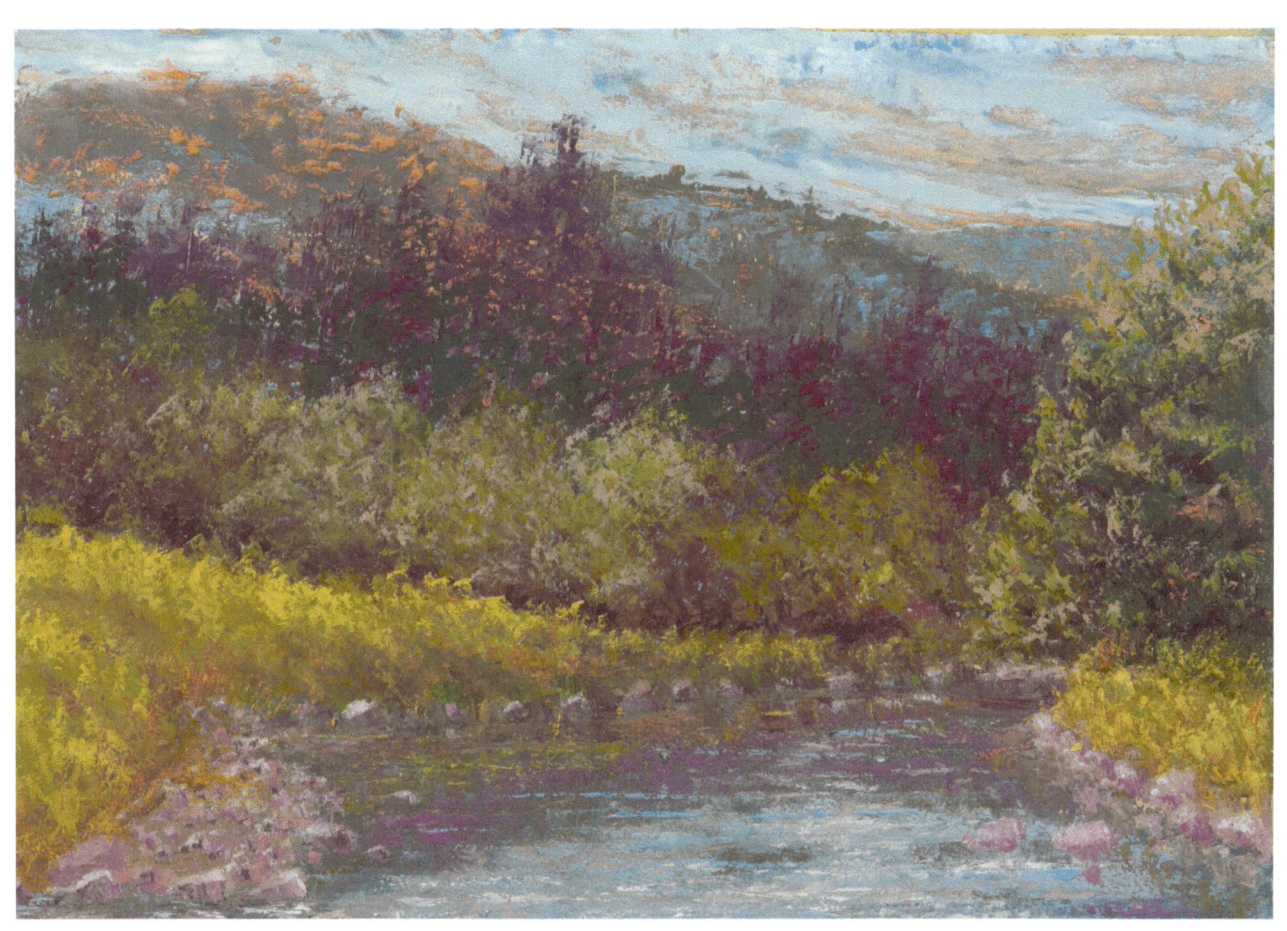

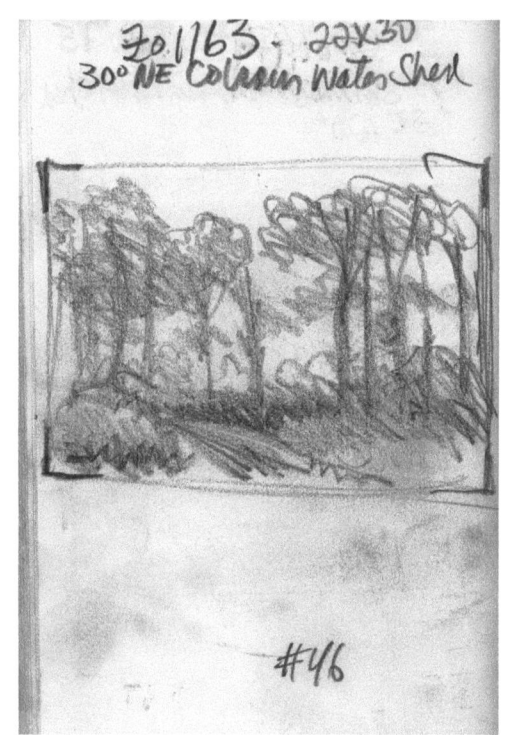

Clearcut, Colrain Watershed

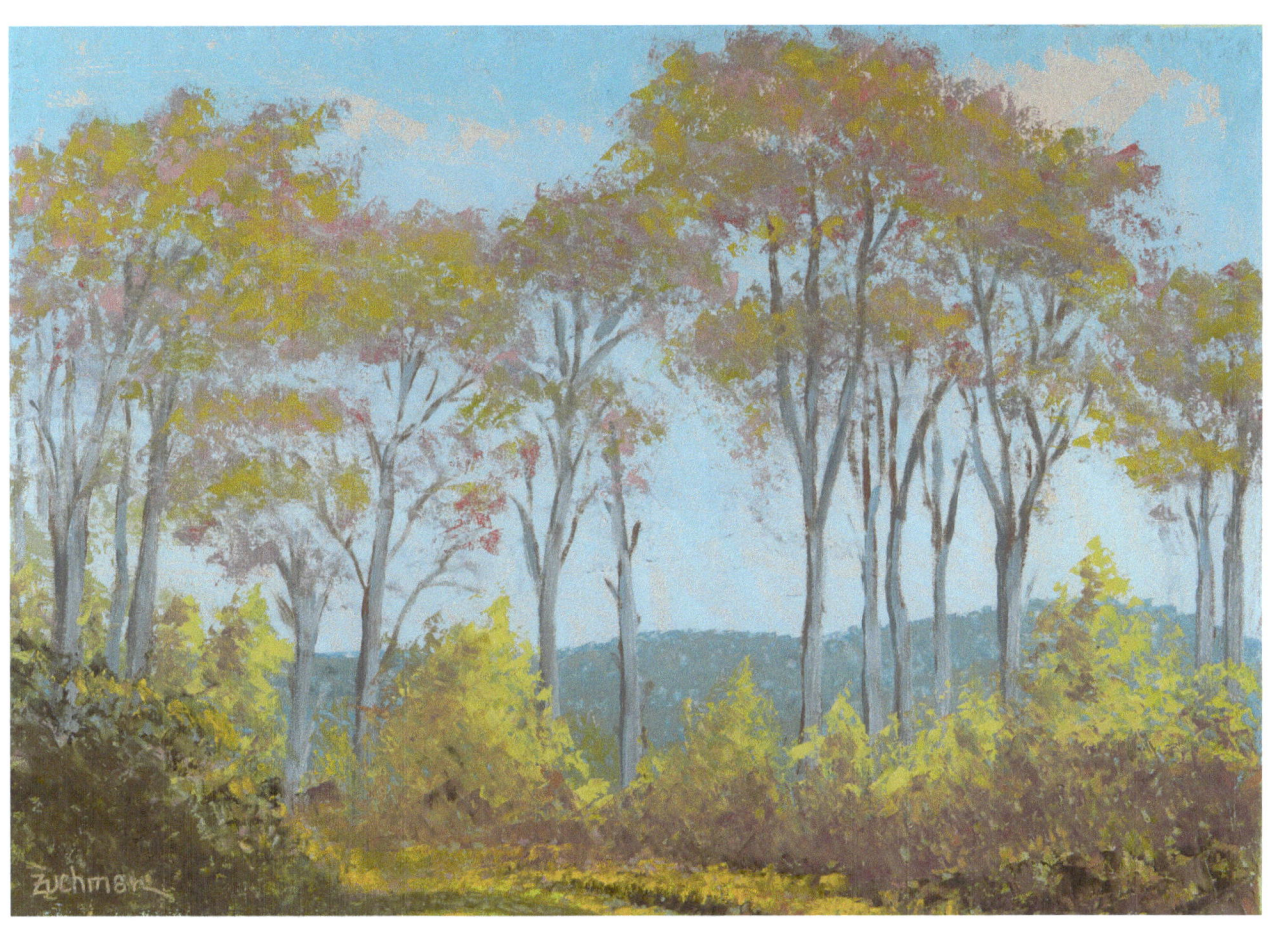

Philip Zuchman

Philip Zuchman is a painter, an explorer and poet, as well as a student of philosophy, psychology and literature.

Born in New York City, he has been on his own since age 14. At 18, he designed, built and paddled a 14-foot kayak 2,000 miles to the Carolina Sea Islands.

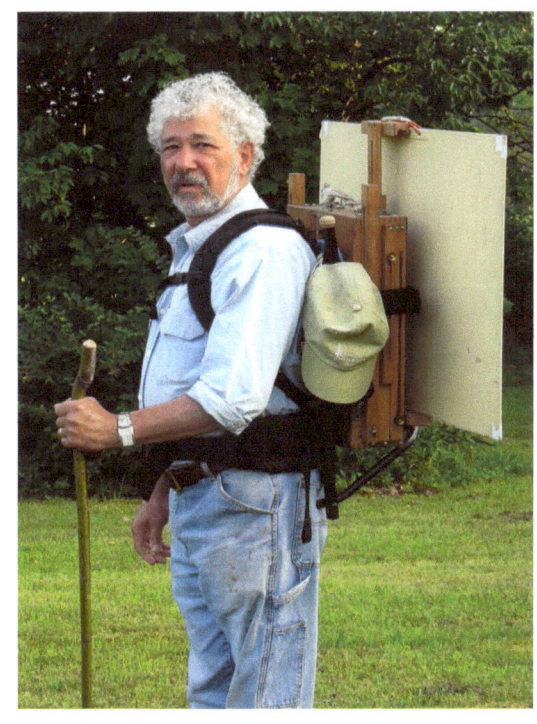

Until the age of 26 he immersed himself in philosophy (B.A. Queens College, CUNY) and writing. He was awarded the Peter Pauper Press Award for two novelettes and had a play, The Gift, produced in Monterrey, California, where he served as a Psychological Research Specialist and French Interpreter in the U.S. Army.

After his military discharge, he returned to Manhattan to paint. He studied at the Art Student's League in 1970 with Arthur Foster. The Salmagundi Club awarded him its Young Artist's Scholarship from 1971-1975.

Zuchman moved to a farm in Walden, Vermont in 1970 and earned his Masters degree in Painting while studying with Jim Gahagan at Goddard College. He then moved to Philadelphia, Pennsylvania.

Zuchman has served as vice president of Artists Equity, Philadelphia and vice president of the Philadelphia Watercolor Society. He is a Professor of Studio Art and Aesthetics at the Art Institute of Philadelphia.

Zuchman lives in West Philadelphia with his wife, painter Deborah Gross-Zuchman. They have painted in Italy, New Mexico, California, New England, Canada, Spain, Colombia and Costa Rica.

SOLO EXHIBITS

2010 **Punti di Vista,** Morrovalle, Macerata, Italy

2006 **De Philadelphia con Amor,** Galleria de Arte Los Commmunes, La Ceja, Colombia

2004 **Visti di Bevagna,** Bevagna, Perugia, Italy

2001 **Cervera Solo Estamos Mirando,** Cervera Del Maestrat, Catalan, Spain

1997 **Spirit into Form,** Brandeis Bardin Institute, Brandeis, California

1993 **New Works,** The Mill Gallery, Philadelphia, Pennsylvania

1991 **Paintings of Mount Monodnock,** The English Gallery, Peterborough, New Hampshire

1988 **Retrospective Exhibition,** Ars et Decora Gallery, Philadelphia, Pennsylvania

SELECTED GROUP EXHIBITS

2012 **Windows and Mirrors,** Continued travelling exhibition from 2010 to 15 American cities

2011 **10th Lessedra World Art Print Annual,** Lessedra Gallery, Sophia, Bulgaria

2011 **Recycling with Imagination,** Viridian Gallery, New York City

2010 **Midyear,** Butler Institute of American Art, Youngstown, Ohio

2009 **Back to Cezanne,** Artists House Gallery, Philadelphia, Pennsylvania

2008 **Small Works,** Artists House Gallery, Philadelphia, Pennsylvania

2006 **Salon Independiente de Arte en el Oriente Antioqueno,**
Galleria Callejon de san Bartolo, Rio Negro, Colombia

2005 **Chapter and Verse,** Travelling exhibit

2005 **Art from Detritus,** Synagogue for the Arts, New York City

2002 **Tres Vistas da Espagna,** Artjaz Gallery, Philadelphia, Pennsylvania

2002 **Snapshot,** Aldrich Museum of Contemporary Art, Ridgefield, Connecticut,
Contemporary Museum, Baltimore, Maryland

2002 **Pai sajos Toxicos,** International Gallery, Biblioteca Nacional, Havana, Cuba

1999 **Artists on Famous Artists,** Brea Civic and Cultural Center, Brea, California

1994 **Rocks, Rills, Woods and Templed Hills,** Goforth Rittenhouse Gallery, Philadelphia

1993 **State of the Art,** The New England Art Institute, Boston, Massachusetts

1991 **The Art of Future Past,** Levy Gallery, Moore College of Art, Philadelphia, Pennsylvania

1987 **Midyear,** Butler Institute of American Art, Youngstown, Ohio

1987 **Woodmere Art Museum Annual,** Chestnut Hill, Pennsylvania

RECOGNITIONS

Professor of Studio Arts and Aesthetics, the Art Institute of Philadelphia

Artists Equity, Philadelphia, Past Vice President and Board of Directors

Philadelphia Water Color Society, Past Vice President and Board of Directors

The Julia and David White Artist Colony, Fellowship, Ciudad Colon, Costa Rica, 2008

The Vermont Studio Center, Artist in Residence, Artist Grant, 2002

The Brandeis Bardin Institute, Artist in Residence, 1997

The Salmagundi Club, Young Artists Scholarship, 1971-1975

"American Cultural Ambassador," U.S. State Department, Art in Embassies Program:
Tirena, Albania ("American Landscapes"); American Institute in Taiwan, China ("Paintings of New England"); Kolonia, Micronesia; San Salvador, El Salvador; Addas Ababa, Ethiopia; Bangui, Central African Republic; Quito, Ecuador; Tegucigalpa, Honduras; Libreville, Gabon; Lagos, Nigeria; Stockholm, Sweden ("World Disarmament Conference")

BIBLIOGRAPHY

Artist Activist, Wendy Weinberg, Director. Video WYBE, Channel 29, 2002

Philip Zuchman: His Life and Art, Tanya Payne, Director, Video, 2000

Outstanding People of the 20th Century, International Biographical Centre, Cambridge, England

Color, American Artist Publications, 1999

After Auschwitz: Responses to the Holocaust in Contemporary Art, Monica Bohm-Duchen, London

A Work in Progress, Susan Saba, the Philadelphia Inquirer, July 1, 1994

The Color Green, Ginny Baier, American Artist Magazine, Spring 1993

Home is Where the Art Is, Stephen Maleson, the Weekly Press, March 25, 1993

Quick Sketch: Philip Zuchman, Joseph Torrano, Art Matters

Philip Zuchman's Work Goes International, University City Review, December 29, 1989

Oil Paintings 2011

Page 7	High Ledges Wildlife Sanctuary	22X30 inches
Page 9	Mount Snow From Patten Hill	22X30 inches
Page 11	The Trail	22X30 inches
Page 13	Apple Orchard at Truesdell's #1	22X30 inches
Page 15	Northeast Vista	22X30 inches
Page 17	Tractor Trail	22X30 inches
Page 19	Above the Watershed	22X30 inches
Page 21	Swamp At Goldswaithe's #1	22X30 inches
Page 23	Sanctuary Meadow #2	15X20 inches
Page 25	Patten Road	22X30 inches
Page 27	Swamp at Goldswaithe's #2,	22X30 inches
Page 29	Pioneer Valley from Florida	22X30 inches
Page 31	In the Mow	22X30 inches
Page 33	Sanctuary Meadow#1	22X30 inches
Page 35	Apple Orchard at Truesdell's #2	22X30 inches
Page 37	Logging Trail at Little Mohawk	30X22 inches
Page 39	Square Lot Road #1	22X30 inches
Page 41	Orcutt Hill, Buckland	22X30 inches
Page 43	Swamp at Goldswaithe's #3	22X30 inches
Page 45	From Frank Williams Road,	22X30 inches
Page 47	Lower Lot at Frankton Road	22X30 inches
Page 49	Raking at Turkey Trees	22X30 inches
Page 51	Soaked in Monochrome	22X30 inches
Page 53	Wheeler Farm	22X30 inches
Page 55	High Ledges in Fog	22X30 inches
Page 57	East From Washer's	22X30 inches
Page 59	Sanctuary Road	30X22 inches
Page 61	Turkey Trees #1	22X30 inches
Page 63	Goldswaithe's South #1	22X30 inches
Page 65	Goldswaithe's South#2	22X30 inches
Page 67	Contra Sol	22X30 inches
Page 69	Square Lot Road #2	15X20 inches
Page 71	Sanctuary Meadow #3	22X30 inches
Page 73	Sunrise, Colrain Watershed	20X15 inches
Page 75	Turkey Trees #2	22X30 inches
Page 77	Topped Trees, Colrain Watershed	22X30 inches
Page 79	The Rocks	15X20 inches
Page 81	Clearcut, Colrain Watershed	22X30 inches